JACQUES COUSTEAU

Conservation Heroes

...tion Heroes

JACQUES COUSTEAU

Johanna Knowles

CHELSEA HOUSE
An Infobase Learning Company

Jacques Cousteau
Copyright ©2011 by Infobase Learning

Chelsea House
An imprint of Infobase Learning
132 West 31st Street
New York, NY 10001

Library of Congress Cataloging-in-Publication Data
Knowles, Johanna (Johanna Beth), 1970–
 Jacques Cousteau / by Johanna Knowles.
  p. cm. — (Conservation heroes)
 Includes bibliographical references and index.
 ISBN 978-1-60413-947-1 (hardcover)
1. Cousteau, Jacques, 1910–1997—Juvenile literature. 2. Oceanographers—
France—Biography—Juvenile literature. I. Title.
 GC30.C68K57 2011
 551.46092—dc22
 [B]   2010030584

Chelsea House books are available at special discounts when purchased in
bulk quantities for businesses, associations, institutions, or sales promotions.
Please call our Special Sales Department in New York at (212) 967-8800 or
(800) 322-8755.

You can find Chelsea House on the World Wide Web
at http://www.chelseahouse.com

Text design by Annie O'Donnell
Cover design by Takeshi Takahashi
Composition by Newgen North America
Cover printed by Bang Printing, Brainerd, MN
Book printed and bound by Bang Printing, Brainerd, MN
Date printed: January 2011
Printed in the United States of America

10 9 8 7 6 5 4 3 2 1

This book is printed on acid-free paper.

All links and Web addresses were checked and verified to be correct at the time
of publication. Because of the dynamic nature of the Web, some addresses and
links may have changed since publication and may no longer be valid.

Contents

From the Skies to the Sea

Jacques Cousteau never intended to be an undersea explorer. As a young man, he wanted to take to the air as a navy flyer, seeing the world from above as he soared through the sky. Still, there were many moments in his childhood that would hint at his true calling.

Jacques had traveled all his life, starting at a young age when his father became a personal lawyer and advisor for a wealthy businessman who required the older Cousteau to travel with him to his various homes in France and the United States. When Jacques was 10 years old, his father moved the family from Paris to New York. At his new American school, Jacques struggled to fit in. Not only did he have to learn a new language, but he had to adapt to a whole new culture. In time, he managed to find a few friends, but he mainly kept to himself. Although his parents worried about his lack of a social life, he didn't seem to mind at all. He was perfectly content playing by himself, inventing mechanical gadgets and later experimenting with a home movie camera he'd saved up money for. By the time he was 16, Jacques had even convinced a handful of

In this photo from the early 1940s, Captain Jacques Cousteau, wearing his French naval uniform, poses with his father and his brother Pierre-Antoine in front of the family home in Paris, France.

friends to join his "production company" and help him film various short movies.

As he became more caught up in his own interests, Jacques grew increasingly frustrated with school life, which he found tedious and boring. He wanted to spend his time on the things that interested him and not be bothered by other school requirements. By the time he reached high school, Jacques was labeled a troublemaker and was expelled after breaking several windows at his school. Worried and frustrated, his parents enrolled him in a strict boarding school in Alsace, France. To everyone's surprise, Jacques thrived in this new environment. He even graduated with honors in 1929. With much relief, his parents celebrated his graduation.

However, Cousteau had no plans to continue his education—at least not the kind that would have him stuck behind a desk for the next several years. He was only 20 years old and wanted to see the world and have adventures. He decided to enroll in the French Naval Academy in Brest, France. Here, he spent two years training, followed by a year-long training cruise around the world. During his training, Cousteau brought his old camera with him and shot as much film footage as he could.

Cousteau graduated as a gunnery officer and joined the French Navy to begin his training as a navy flyer. He had always enjoyed traveling and especially loved flying. Now, he'd chosen a career that would allow him to do both. Life was going just as he'd planned. Then, one summer night in 1933, everything changed.

Cousteau borrowed his father's sports car to go to a friend's wedding in the Vosges Mountains. On the way, the roads were twisting and narrow. It was dark, but Cousteau was a confident driver. Suddenly, though, his car lights dimmed. He failed to see that he'd come to a sharp, hairpin curve in the road. Everything went dark. When he opened his eyes, he found himself trapped in his car, bleeding and in severe pain. The tiny sports car had careened into a retaining wall. There was nothing he could do but wait and hope someone would find him and get him to the hospital in time.

(continues on page 12)

A WHOLE NEW WORLD

As a child at a summer camp in Vermont, Cousteau liked to open his eyes while he was swimming underwater to see what he could of the mysterious, silent world below the surface of the water. Swimming in the sea, however, was different because the salt water stung his eyes and blurred his vision. As he got older, he focused on his strengths as a swimmer and forgot about the underwater world beneath him.

All that changed one morning in 1936 at Le Mourillon, a small, seaside town located on the Mediterranean Sea, near Toulon, France, where he was stationed in the navy. It was here, that Cousteau met Phillip Tailliez, a fellow navy officer. The two became fast friends and spent much of their free time at the beach, swimming and fishing. One day, Cousteau got his hands on a pair of Fernez goggles. He'd heard many stories about fishermen who used them to catch fish under the water, and he wanted to try them for himself. He slipped them on, waded into the cool, salty water, and dipped his head below the surface. "I was astounded by what I saw in the shallow shingle at Le Mourillon," he writes in his first book, *The Silent World*. "Rocks covered with green, brown and silver forests of algae and fishes unknown to me, swimming in crystalline water."

This was Cousteau's first taste of life under the sea, and he immediately became starved for more. He knew from that moment on that his life had changed. He began to think about developing an apparatus that would allow him to stay underwater longer and see even more of this mysterious world.

After two years of diving with only goggles, he met another diver, Frédéric Dumas, who shared his love of swimming and diving.

Jacques Cousteau uses scuba gear as he studies fish in the depths of the Indian Ocean.

Cousteau, Dumas, and Tailliez became a close diving trio and constantly talked about ways they could improve swimming and diving. The men came up with various techniques for breathing while their heads were submerged underwater. They got quite creative, even using lengths of garden hose, putting one end of the hose in their mouth while the other end stuck out of the water, just like a modern-day snorkel.

Still, devices like this hardly sufficed. Cousteau and his friends continued to brainstorm until eventually they came up with an invention that would revolutionize recreational swimming and exploring. They called this new invention a self-contained underwater breathing apparatus. Its name was eventually shortened to *scuba* gear.

(continued from page 9)

For the next three days, Cousteau drifted in and out of consciousness. Finally, he opened his eyes to the bright lights of a hospital room. He could not remember what had happened.

He soon learned that the news wasn't good. Cousteau had broken 12 bones in his body and was lucky to be alive at all. If it hadn't been for a local farmer who happened by shortly after the crash, he might have bled to death. Luckily, his life had been spared, but the course of his future had been changed forever.

Cousteau's arms were badly injured. His left arm was broken in five places. His right arm was badly infected and paralyzed and his doctor told him the safest way to prevent further complications would be to amputate it. Yet Cousteau refused to accept this diagnosis. Even after the doctor told him the risks of not having an amputation, he refused to go ahead with the procedure and said that he'd rather die than live without his arm. Reluctantly, the doctor relented and treated the wound as well as he could. To everyone's surprise, Cousteau recovered.

Nevertheless, Cousteau's dreams of becoming a pilot were over. As he healed slowly, his arms remained very weak, and he suffered a lot of pain. To gain his strength back, he took to the water. He swam gently at first, working on strengthening his arms. The more time he spent in the water, the more he began to take notice of the sea in which he swam. He'd always loved swimming as a child, but now, diving deep into the depths and discovering the beauty below the surface, he wanted to see more. He wondered if he could stay underwater longer, dive deeper, and explore further.

Cousteau had no idea then that these questions would set him on a new course that would change his life dramatically. While his dreams of becoming a flyer had been dashed, he had found a new calling. He decided to continue his work in the navy. However, instead of focusing on the sky above, he started focusing on the sea below. The more time he spent underwater, the longer he wanted to stay there. For the rest of his life, he would work on developing new machines that would help him go deeper and stay underwater longer. Working with other engineers, he would invent new devices for swimming underwater and, later, filming underwater, too.

COUSTEAU'S WINDOW

The more he saw of the beauty of life underwater, the more Cousteau wanted to share his discoveries with others. He still loved photography and film and decided to try filming underwater. It took many tries, but he finally managed to build a waterproof case for his camera. Underwater filmmaking was born.

After his career in the navy, Cousteau devoted his life to filming underwater sea life. He leased an old boat that had been used as a mine-sweeper in World War II that he called *Calypso*. Along with his crew, Cousteau re-outfitted the boat to accommodate their diving and filming needs. Cousteau, his wife Simone, his two sons, and his crew made *Calypso* their home for years to come as they sailed over seas, up canals and rivers, and anywhere else they felt drawn to.

Cousteau's first films won major awards and led to one of the most popular educational television series in history. Beginning in 1966, viewers from around the world tuned in to watch Cousteau and his team swim underwater alongside dolphins, whales, sharks, octopuses, and other mysterious creatures. Cousteau's films opened a window to a whole new world, and viewers couldn't get enough. In addition, Cousteau and his crew explored sunken ships and their treasures, thrilling the world with their discoveries. Never before had people seen images of underwater sea life and its treasures as they did through Cousteau's lenses. Because of these films, new generations would develop a love for the sea and an appreciation for creatures and plant life. This era was an exciting time for everyone, but especially for Cousteau and his family.

EXPLORER TURNED CONSERVATIONIST

The more Cousteau traveled, the more amazing discoveries he found. His observations of sea life that had never been seen by human eyes sparked worldwide interest in the underwater world. Still, as he traveled the world's seas and waterways, he became aware of another important issue: The oceans and seas were in grave danger, thanks to the effects of pollution, overfishing, and human overpopulation on sea creatures, plant life, and water quality in general.

Cousteau wondered: How could he protect the silent world he loved? The answer, again, was film. By showing the world life under the sea, he'd also inspired tremendous love for it. If he used his films to show the damages of pollution, maybe his viewers would be inspired to change how humans treated the oceans.

Cousteau got to work. One film showed how a coral reef in the Mediterranean had been changed for the worse in just 10 years by

NO DUMPING!

In 1960, Cousteau learned that the French Commission of Atomic Energy (*Commissariat á l'énergie atomique,* also known as the CEA), had plans to dump radioactive waste into the Mediterranean Sea. Cousteau was outraged. He'd seen firsthand what pollution was doing to the sea life in many parts of the world. He also had a particular love for the Mediterranean, where he'd swam as a child and where his career had blossomed. Atomic waste, he knew, could have devastating effects on plants and animals for decades to come.

Cousteau organized a campaign to protest the dump, drawing support from people of all ages. Protesters lined the tracks to block the train that was carrying the waste from reaching the sea. Some worried whether the train would actually stop, but, in the end, the protest succeeded: The train stopped and turned around. This protest also initiated an important discussion about radioactive waste and its effect on the environment.

overfishing and pollution. The film stunned the world into action. Cousteau talked to fishermen and explained how if they continued to fish without restrictions, soon there would be no fish left to catch. They listened and changed the way they did business. It seemed the more popular Cousteau became, the more people started to care about the health of the sea. Soon, a worldwide movement started to protect the Earth's oceans.

SPOKESPERSON FOR THE SEA

Cousteau became a beloved and trusted guide to the sea. He inspired people to take action on its behalf. For decades, he combined entertainment and conservation education to help protect the seas he loved. He would become one of the most famous and revered conservationists in history. He would inspire thousands of young people to pursue education and careers in marine studies and conservation. Even now, people from all over the world visit the market village of St.-André-de-Cubzac, France, where Cousteau was born, to pay tribute to the statue placed there in his memory: a large wooden dolphin, carved to look as if it is jumping out of the sea with a red knit cap in its mouth, a cap just like the ones that Cousteau and his crew wore on *Calypso*.

Cousteau's Early Years: Proving Them Wrong

Jacques-Yves Cousteau was born on June 11, 1910 in Saint-André-de-Cubzac, Gironde, France. His parents were Daniel and Élizabeth Cousteau. He had a brother, Pierre-Antoine, who was four years older than him. During Jacques's first years, his parents traveled to accommodate his father's job as an assistant to an American businessman named James Hazen Hyde. Hyde liked to travel and had business contacts all over the world. He required that Daniel Cousteau accompany him on these travels. Often, the elder Cousteau brought his family along, especially if they were to stay at one place for an extended time. This life seemed to work well for the young Cousteau family. However, World War I broke out and everything changed.

When the German army reached France in 1914, the French government retreated to the city of Bordeaux. Hyde and the Cousteaus were in Paris at this time and living there ceased to be a luxurious adventure. James Hyde decided to go back to the United States and fired Daniel Cousteau. The elder Cousteau now had to fend for himself and his family. Luckily, Élizabeth Cousteau had some family money, which they used to get by in Paris for the next several years of the war.

At the same time, Jacques developed several health problems. He had started out as a happy, healthy baby, but suddenly he began to have stomach problems, including chronic enteritis (an inflammation of the small intestine). People thought of him as a sickly child because he was so pale and uncomfortable. Meanwhile, the family was having a harder and harder time finding enough food to eat. Finally, they decided to return to Élizabeth Cousteau's family home in Saint-André-de-Cubzac. There, they lived off the vegetables they grew in the family gardens. Living in the country, however, failed to improve Jacques's health or demeanor. As he grew, he remained a quiet boy. He didn't have much interest in playing with other children at sports or other games. What did seem to make him the happiest, however, was playing alone and building structures with sticks and rocks he found outdoors. His parents became increasingly worried about his anti-social behavior.

TO AMERICA

After World War I ended in 1918, Parisian life began to flourish again. Daniel Cousteau met another wealthy American, Eugene Higgins, who hired him as his assistant and advisor. Higgins owned homes in both New York and Paris and liked to travel back and forth between them at different times of the year. He required Daniel Cousteau to accompany him. Not wanting to leave his wife and children for such long, extended periods, Jacques's father decided to move them with him.

The Cousteau family's first voyage to New York, on a French Line ship, took eight days, and young Jacques Cousteau, now 10 years old, had the time of his life. He enjoyed exploring every inch of the ship and following the crew around. He would ask them endless questions about how the ship worked, what sailing life was like, and anything else he could think of. Jacques also loved peeking into the cabins, staring out at the sea, and living onboard in general. The crew was taken with his enthusiasm and happy to share their knowledge with him. This change in behavior shocked and pleased his parents, who for so long had worried about their quiet, anti-social son. Perhaps this move would be just the thing their son needed.

Unfortunately, his sociability wore off when it became obvious how difficult it was going to be to adjust to life in the United States, where few people spoke French and fewer seemed to want to welcome Jacques into their group of friends. More and more, young Cousteau looked to his older brother Pierre-Antoine as a role model and someone to emulate. Pierre-Antoine, who was nicknamed "PAC," was in high school at the time. Jacques started calling himself "Jack" because it sounded more American and rhymed with his brother's nickname.

The best thing about American schools, the boys thought, was that they weren't nearly as strict and challenging as the schools they'd attended in France. While both boys learned the language fairly quickly, Jacques was never able to find his own group of friends and saw PAC as his only true friend. Again, his parents worried about his lack of a social life. Meanwhile, his father was so busy traveling around the United States with his new boss, he was rarely home. Both Cousteau brothers became afraid that their mother might enroll them in boarding school so that she could travel with their father, so they worked hard to make her happy so that she would want to stay home with them.

FRIENDLESS BUT CONTENT

At school, young Cousteau continued to fall behind in sports and other physical activities. He often got winded quickly and was seen as a boy who was easy to beat. However, this didn't seem to bother him for long. Instead, he chose to spend time on the activities that did interest him, mainly building and inventing.

When he was 11 years old, Jacques received a copy of *Popular Mechanics* magazine. In it, he discovered instructions on how to build a crane. He was delighted and quickly gathered all the supplies he needed to build his own crane. He also decided to add his own features to the original design to make it even more useful. When he was finished, the crane was as tall as he was and could

THE DARKER SIDE OF PIERRE-ANTOINE ("PAC") COUSTEAU (1906–1958)

When Jacques Cousteau was 12, his brother PAC was 16 and through with school. He had no interest in going to college and convinced his father to allow him to quit high school a year before graduation. There would be no university education for PAC, who was eager to get his military service over with so that he could become a wealthy businessman like those for whom his father worked. However, while he was serving in the military, PAC became interested in French politics. He believed in the need for reforms that would help the working class. He came to believe that French society was corrupt and inhumane. He thought it was unfair of the government to ask France's middle- and lower-class young men to fight while its policies treated them so unfairly. After he finished his military service, he worked as a translator and then as a meteorologist. Eventually, he became politically active as a Communist and became a reporter for left-wing newspapers as he pursued his interest in politics.

In the 1930s, PAC gave up on Communism and turned to right-wing politics, especially anti-Semitism. He also spoke out against democracy and traveled to Nazi Germany to learn more about Nazism. Even though he did not officially become a Nazi, he supported their campaign against the Jews during World War II. After the war, he fled to Switzerland where he was arrested and condemned to death. His sentence was later commuted to life in prison with hard labor. In 1954, he was released from prison as part of an amnesty agreement. He died four years later in Paris at the age of 52.

slide back and forth on the rolling cams (rotating pieces) that he added himself. When his father came home and saw the crane, he was so impressed that he told an engineer friend about it. The friend thought it was so amazing that he suggested they apply for a patent. While the Cousteaus didn't follow this suggestion, this display of Jacques's talent helped to reassure his parents that he had a bright future. Still, they were worried about his lack of friends.

That summer, Jacques's parents sent him to summer camp, thinking that maybe being around children his own age in a fun setting would make it easier for him to make friends. Unfortunately, things didn't work out quite as they hoped. On the first day of camp, the campers were introduced to horseback riding. Jacques knew right away that this wasn't going to be for him, but he gave it a try. Almost as soon as he mounted, the horse threw him off. Jacques wanted to give up on horseback riding right there, but the riding instructor forced him to get back in the saddle. Sitting there, Jacques looked around at the other campers, who were staring at him. He felt like a failure, but he was also angry at the instructor for making him do something he didn't want to. He dismounted and refused to ride. The instructor became furious: How dare this young boy disobey him? Nevertheless, Jacques stubbornly stood his ground.

As punishment, the instructor ordered Jacques to clear all the dead branches out of the swimming pond. The pond was dark, muddy, and the bottom was invisible. Scary stories about the deep, dark pond were often spread around the camp. Still, Jacques took a deep breath as he eased himself under the water. The first thing he noticed when he opened his eyes and looked around was the quiet. There were no horses, no yelling counselors, and no sneering boys—just peaceful water all around. He went to work hauling out the dead branches from the pond, each time diving underwater to the calm, silent world below.

BACK TO FRANCE

When he turned 12, Jacques's life changed dramatically again when his father's boss decided to move back to Paris and to take

Young Jacques Cousteau was thrilled to buy a used Pathé Baby camera, shown in this 1920s advertisement. The hand-cranked camera enabled him to begin making movies.

Cousteau's father with him. Thus, the Cousteau family packed their things and traveled back to France. They hadn't been back long when PAC decided to leave home for military service. Because Daniel traveled so much, this left Jacques home alone with his mother. By now, he was entering his teen years and having an even more difficult time fitting in at school. He felt uncomfortable with his looks (he thought he had a big nose) and still didn't know how to make friends. He spent a lot of time alone in his room, working with various models and machines and reading about new inventions.

One day, he came across an article about a movie camera. During the 1920s, going to the cinema was all the rage, and Jacques was fascinated by the movies as much as everyone else. He read everything he could about cameras, fascinated by their mechanics. For months, he saved his money until he could finally afford to buy a used Pathé Baby, a hand-cranked camera used to make home movies. Almost as soon as Jacques got the camera home, he began to study how it was made and how it worked. He even took it apart and put it back together again—more than once. Everything about film fascinated him, including the chemical processes used to develop film. He loved how taking several still shots in a row could make a moving picture.

A PASSION FOR FILM IS BORN

Jacques spent all of his free time experimenting with the camera. He managed to gather a small troupe of movie enthusiasts to join him in making short films. These were probably his first friends and he was having the time of his life. His schoolwork, however, was suffering from all the fun. His grades plummeted, and he became more rebellious. Finally, his mother took matters into her own hands and took the camera away from her son. Jacques responded by becoming more rebellious than ever, even breaking school windows, an act for which he was suspended. Jacques's parents were at their wits' end and finally decided to enroll him in a very strict boarding school—without his camera.

To everyone's surprise, rather than being miserable in his new environment, Jacques thrived and graduated at the top of his class. When he returned home, however, he still needed to decide what to do with this life. He decided to fulfill his childhood dream of flying by applying to the French Naval Academy. His training took him around the world on a training ship. His seagoing experiences would later inspire his interest in making films about it.

Young Simone Melchior was introduced to Jacques Cousteau by her father. They married in Paris the following year when Simone was 18.

After he graduated, Cousteau joined the French Navy, where he trained to become a navy pilot and looked forward to a career full of excitement, travel, and adventure in the air. However, in

SIMONE THE SHEPHERDESS: SIMONE MELCHIOR COUSTEAU (1919–1990)

Born in 1919 to parents Henri and Marguerite Melchior, Simone Melchior had an upbringing similar to her future husband's. Her family traveled often when she was a child and so she developed a strong sense of adventure. She and Cousteau were as much business partners as they were husband and wife. On board *Calypso,* a boat she helped Cousteau find and acquire, she played many roles. She often acted as mother to the crew, which numbered up to 30. She cooked for them, cut their hair, and acted as nurse whenever anyone became sick or injured. She was even known to break up fights! Her talent for keeping the men together earned her the nickname "*La Bergère,*" which is French for "The Shepherdess."

In the early days, Simone Cousteau was so determined to make *Calypso* a success that she sold her family jewels and fur coats to pay for fuel and to equip the boat with a compass and gyroscope. Often, when Jacques Cousteau needed to leave the boat to give talks, attend meetings, or do film and book promotions, Simone was left in charge. Her older son, Jean-Michel, claimed she was the real captain of *Calypso* because she spent more time on board than Jacques Cousteau and her two sons combined. After she died in 1990, her ashes were scattered in the Mediterranean Sea.

the summer of 1933, just as he was about to earn his pilot's wings, tragedy struck. Cousteau's life-changing car crash ended his pilot's career.

Simone Cousteau was instrumental in many of her husband's early successes. She introduced him to an engineer and fund-raisers who would help him co-invent the Aqua-Lung and sold her family jewels and fur coats to purchase *Calypso*'s fuel, compass, and gyroscope in the ship's early days.

MEETING SIMONE

By the summer of 1936, Cousteau still hadn't fully recovered from his accident. He could move his arms well enough to swim and hold a camera, but it sometimes hurt. That summer, he'd been having fun doing more experiments with film and took his camera with him everywhere he went. One evening, he was invited to a cocktail party hosted by a woman named Marguerite Melchior, who was throwing the party in hopes of introducing her 17-year-old daughter Simone to eligible French Navy men.

Cousteau noticed Simone the moment he walked through the door, but he decided to play it cool and chatted with another woman instead. Simone, however, had noticed Cousteau, too. She liked his quirky looks and bright smile. She also thought it was strange that he had brought his movie camera with him to a cocktail party—and it seemed even more brazen of him to start filming the guests! She wondered: Who was this mysterious young man? They both kept their eyes on each other all night, becoming more and more attracted and curious as the evening continued.

Finally, Simone's father, Admiral Henri Melchior, began to notice the looks passing between his daughter and Cousteau and decided to take action. He led Simone over to Cousteau and made a proper introduction. Melchior explained that Cousteau had been in an auto accident recently and Cousteau told her what happened. The two found it easy to talk together, even though Cousteau, at 26, was 9 years older than Simone. Both immediately felt that they had found their soul mate. They spent the rest of the evening together, discovering all the things they had in common. Like Cousteau, Simone had grown up traveling with her parents, loved to explore new places, and, maybe most importantly, she also loved adventure. Plus, she came from a navy family, while Cousteau was himself a navy man. Over the following year, the two of them got together as often as they could. Then, in the summer of 1937, following Simone's graduation from high school, the couple was married.

Cousteau and the Invention of the Aqua-Lung

In 1936, before the Cousteaus were married, Jacques Cousteau was still stationed in Toulon, France. At that time, he was still undergoing therapy for his arms, which were continuing to slowly heal from his car crash. The therapy was very painful, and Cousteau became impatient to get well. Since he could no longer be a flyer, the navy reassigned him as a gunnery officer. Often by the end of the day, Cousteau was completely exhausted. Finally, Cousteau's friend, Philippe Tailliez, took him aside for a talk. Tailliez was a respected officer and a bit older than Cousteau, and Cousteau respected him and listened to his advice. He suggested to Cousteau that regular swimming might strengthen his arms. Desperate to try anything that might help, Cousteau agreed. The two set out for the rocky beach of Sanary-sur-Mer, near Toulon, the next day.

THE HEALING SEA

Cousteau was surprised and excited to discover that Tailliez was an impressive and inventive swimmer. In fact, since his childhood,

Tailliez had been inventing ways to swim faster, dive deeper, and explore the underwater. His first fins were made from pieces of metal saw blades that he strapped between two slabs of rubber and tied to his feet with baling twine! Tailliez also experimented with underwater goggles made from cloth and glass panes, and a snorkel he made out of a garden hose. Cousteau was fascinated and delighted with both Tailliez's diving skills and inventions. After their first swimming excursion, they began to meet every day. Tailliez would hunt fish with a handmade spear while Cousteau swam to strengthen his arms.

One day, Tailliez suggested that Cousteau try out his mask and goggles. Up to then, he was convinced that the only thing worth knowing about the salty seawater was how to swim in it in case he ever had to abandon ship without a life raft. Now, at Tailliez's insistence, Cousteau put on the gear. He swam out from shore, trying to understand how the strange snorkel worked. From there, he gradually ducked underwater, until finally his view of everything changed. Cousteau was mesmerized by what he saw. Far from the murky pond water he remembered from his childhood camp days, the sea was an endless world of dazzling plant and fish life that had been existing unseen all this time while he'd been swimming above it! "Sometimes we are lucky enough to know that our lives have been changed," Cousteau wrote in *The Silent World,* "to discard the old, embrace the new, and run headlong down an immutable course. It happened to me at Le Mourillon on that summer's day, when my eyes were opened on the sea."

Tailliez and Cousteau became underwater swimmates, diving, fishing, and exploring. They constantly discussed ways that would help them stay underwater longer. They dreamed of equipment that would give them the freedom to go deeper without experiencing discomfort. To help with this question, Cousteau began to study the molecular structure of water. He studied mass, as well, and learned about water pressure and ocean depth. He immersed himself in everything to do with the sea and diving, which was then called skin diving.

FILMING IN THE SEA

After a year of swimming with Tailliez, Cousteau's arms were nearly pain-free. He and Simone had bought a house closer to the sea and enjoyed having guests who also loved to dive. At this time, Cousteau had also begun to think about his earlier love of film and how he could combine it with his new-found love of diving. While Tailliez continued fishing, Cousteau became more occupied with trying to figure out how he could shoot films underwater. He spent one winter coming up with various possibilities for how this would work. By the time the sea warmed up in the spring, Cousteau was ready to test his ideas.

Cousteau bought a used 8 mm movie camera and attached it to a handmade bracket that could fit inside a gallon-sized fruit jar. He then set the camera so that it would record for 30 seconds. Next, Cousteau dove 20 feet (6 meters) underwater and aimed the camera upward at Simone who was swimming on the surface above. He let the camera do the work and hoped for good results.

Back at home, Cousteau developed the film in a darkroom he had set up in his bathroom. He and Simone anxiously awaited the results. Finally, when the film was ready, Cousteau held it in front of the light. There, he saw tiny images of Simone swimming in contrast to the sunlight above. Success! Though he wasn't yet absolutely positive, he thought he may have just made the very first underwater film—and he was ecstatic.

THE SEA MUSKETEERS

In the summer of 1938, Cousteau and Tailliez met a new companion, Fréderic Dumas. Dumas was swimming one day when he observed Tailliez diving and fishing. He referred to Tailliez as a "manfish" who never needed to lift his head out of the water to breathe. Dumas introduced himself to Tailliez who told him all about his equipment and how he made it. He then invited Dumas to come diving with him and Cousteau. From that moment, the three became a well-known trio. They even called themselves *Les Mousquemers* ("The Sea Musketeers"). They loved to go "undersea hunting" and filming with Cousteau's camera. They talked constantly about how to perfect their diving equipment.

The Sea Musketeers were especially interested in finding a way to stay warm so they could stay underwater longer. They experimented by covering themselves with grease, but this covering just washed away and, in fact, left an oily residue that made their bodies lose heat even faster. Finally, Cousteau got the idea of using some sort of rubber suit to hold in body heat. Unfortunately, they encountered several problems with this. One problem with a rubber suit was that it made the diver very buoyant. Also, if air pockets developed inside the suit, it made the suit even harder to maneuver in, and worse, could flip the diver over sideways or on his head. While the three were highly amused when this happened, it also made them feel increasingly frustrated. However, Cousteau was sure there was a solution. All his life, rather than giving up on a task because it "couldn't be done," he only became more interested in finding a solution—and inventing his own if one didn't yet exist.

At the time, there were few options available for breathing underwater if you didn't want to be tethered to a boat above that could deliver oxygen through a tube running from a tank on the vessel to the diver. The most common method involved carrying oxygen in a tank, which was usually strapped to the chest. The diver would then control a valve on the tank which allowed oxygen to pass through a tube to the diver's mouth. This method was cumbersome and made swimming difficult. It also still didn't allow divers to spend much time underwater, and, worst of all, it was very dangerous.

WORLD WAR II

In 1939, war broke out and the Sea Musketeers were separated due to their various duties to help the war effort. Jacques and Simone Cousteau had welcomed their first son, Jean-Michel, into the world a year earlier. Not long after, Jean-Michel would have a brother, Philippe. Cousteau secretly worked for the French Resistance, for which he would receive a French medal of honor.

SMALL ADVENTURERS

Jacques and Simone Cousteau's children were born into a life of adventure—from watching their parents perfect ambitious inventions, traveling through war-torn France, and eventually living at sea on board *Calypso.* Jean-Michel was born in 1938 and Philippe in 1940. Jean-Michel followed in his father's footsteps; Philippe graduated from the French national film school and became a cameraman for the Conshelf III project, the third in a series of underwater living experiments.

When they were boys, they were sent to boarding school, but enjoyed summers traveling with their parents. As adults, both worked closely with their father on various business ventures, but particularly with Cousteau's films, which both appeared in at different times.

The Cousteau family poses in Sanary, France, in the mid-1940s. Shown are (*left to right*) Cousteau's wife Simone, son Philippe, Cousteau (in the car), nephew Jean-Pierre, son Jean-Michel, an unidentified family member, niece Françoise, and mother Élizabeth.

The Sea Musketeers were reunited during the winter of 1941. Cousteau and Tailliez had both been assigned to watch over the fleet at Toulon in the South of France. Dumas joined them there after a harrowing escape in the French Alps. He'd been driving for the army when his unit surrendered to the Germans. Dumas

Cousteau and his family spent a good deal of time on the beach. Shown here in Sanary, France, in the mid-1940s are (*left to right*) Cousteau's nephew Jean-Pierre, son Jean-Michel, Cousteau (in French naval dress), wife Simone, and son Philippe.

escaped through the mountains on foot to safety. Together again, the three of them took to fishing, this time more to feed themselves and their families than for sport. Everyone lived under tight food rations and the fish were a welcome change in their diet.

Cousteau worked for naval intelligence during this period. His commanding officer knew about his diving skills and how they might help with certain missions. He encouraged Cousteau to continue experimenting with underwater filming and breathing methods in order to do secret work, possibly by swimming close to enemy fleets undetected and collecting valuable military intelligence using his camera. At the time, they were concerned that the Germans would occupy nearby Italy and so any information they could gain would help. Outside of their commanding officers, no one suspected the three divers who were constantly bringing home fish from their diving expeditions were actually performing experiments that would help the war effort.

The Sea Musketeers first experimented with a Fernez diving apparatus that worked by carrying air from a pump above water down through a pipe to the diver. The pipe was set across the diver's face to a valve that looked like a duck beak. It provided a constant flow of the air pumped down from above. While it was safer than using an oxygen tank, it was still cumbersome, and required the diver to be tethered to the equipment above. Undeterred by the limits of this approach, the team kept brainstorming.

A NEW KIND OF CAMERA

In addition to his work on the challenges of underwater breathing, Cousteau also worked on developing his filming techniques. In the spring of 1941, he purchased a used 35 mm Kinamo camera at a junk shop. It was so cheap that it didn't even have a lens. A new friend of Cousteau's, Leon Veche, helped him make new housing for the camera that would keep the camera dry when Cousteau took it underwater. The housing was made of metal, and it had a rubber seal. Another friend, Papa Heinic, ground a new lens for the camera.

Cousteau now had a one-of-a-kind underwater camera. With its large film, it would be able to produce sharper images than Cousteau's original 8 mm camera. The only problem was that there wasn't any movie film available. However, there was plenty of still film. So, he and Simone bought what they could and spliced the film themselves, making 50-foot (15.2-m) reels that would produce up to three minutes of film. This took careful, time-consuming work, but both were so excited about the possible results, they hardly noticed. Before testing the camera, Cousteau and his friends spent two weeks perfecting the housing they'd made to make sure it was airtight and the camera would be safe inside. To test the housing without risking harm to the camera, they replaced the camera with half a brick in the housing, which was sealed with jute covered in tar. Together, the camera and housing weighed 20 pounds (9 kilograms) out of the water.

When they were convinced the housing was waterproof, the Cousteaus and their two sons, along with Dumas, Tailliez, and Veche went to the seashore for the first test. The adults excitedly waded in up to their waists, gathering around Cousteau as he carefully lowered the box containing the camera below the water. He then squeezed the trigger mechanism to begin filming. After he was done, they all rushed back to shore and opened the box. To everyone's delight, the camera had stayed dry!

For the next several hours, Cousteau swam farther out and deeper down with the camera. He experimented with the camera controls while learning to swim with the awkward housing. At last he felt ready to really test the camera's limits—he dove down 60 feet (18 meters) and anxiously checked the camera to see if it could handle the pressure. It could.

While the camera and its housing seemed full of promise, however, there would be technical problems. Shortly after the first successful dive, the seals on the housing leaked. Fearing all their hard work was destroyed, Cousteau brought the camera home and took it and its housing apart. He carefully washed every single part—the gears, ratchets, springs, and anything else made of metal—to keep the salty sea water from damaging any metal parts. After all the parts were completely dry, Veche helped Cousteau reassemble the camera. All was fine. Now that they knew how to take the camera apart and clean it and put it together again whenever water got inside, Cousteau felt ready to make his first underwater film.

Underwater Filmmaking is Born

Cousteau's idea for making an underwater film was simple and straightforward: He would film a diver fishing while armed with a spear. This way, the film would be telling a story, while also showing the beauty and wonder of the silent underwater world to those who had never seen it. True to Cousteau's plan, in the film, the diver wears a mask, snorkel, and fins while also carrying a spear gun. The film shows the diver making two attempts before hitting his mark. He then struggles to the surface with his prey.

The most impressive thing about the filming itself was that Cousteau filmed by going underwater and holding his breath without using a breathing apparatus. He had tried to use the Fernez gear, but the bubbles that were released from the mask were scaring away the fish he needed to catch on film. The filming process was extremely slow—painfully so. It took the Sea Musketeers six months to finish their film as they took turns holding the camera and acting. As divers, they hunted and swam and sometimes just made silly faces at the camera. As filmmakers, they shot as much sea life as they could, including fish and plants. Finally, they were ready to edit the film. They learned how to cut and splice, which is necessary to make scenes and create a storytelling sequence that makes sense and is interesting to the viewers.

The film was ready in October 1942 and was titled *Dix-huit Metres de Fond* ("Ten Fathoms Down"). Their first audience was a group of German officers and French politicians from Vichy, France, in occupied Paris. While Cousteau himself was against the Germans and Vichy government, he took his brother PAC's advice to show the film in order to get whatever audience he could. It was PAC who made the showing—as well as a reception afterward—possible.

Shortly after the film's debut, Cousteau and his family were in Marseille, France. Cousteau had been sent as a naval attaché and brought along his wife and sons. One night, the Cousteaus were sleeping peacefully in their hotel room when they heard the loud rumble of planes overhead. It was November 27, 1942. When they turned on the radio, they heard the frightening news that Hitler was invading southern France. By morning, tanks were plowing through the streets. The French Navy quickly destroyed as much of its Mediterranean fleet as it could before the German and Italian forces could seize them for their own use. Battleships, minesweepers, tankers, and cruisers were burned, including *Dupleix,* the ship on which Cousteau served. In the end, the Germans were only able to seize a single destroyer, a torpedo boat, six tankers, tugs, minesweepers, and transport ships.

The navy canceled Cousteau's assignment and ordered him to go to Toulon with his camera to film as much as he could of the devastation. He had Simone and his sons prepare to flee to Paris where they could stay with Élizabeth Cousteau and PAC—who was now writing for a pro-occupation magazine. Cousteau began to use his camera to film for an undercover assignment, gathering as much information about the German and Italian troops as possible. He wore a stolen Italian uniform and entrenched himself among the soldiers, secretly filming whatever he could. He even managed to film maps that highlighted where gun emplacements were. Later, he was awarded France's highest military honor, the Légion d'honneur (Legion of Honor), for his bravery.

BREATHING UNDERWATER

By the time Cousteau was reunited with his wife and children, Simone had already begun searching for a new method of breathing underwater. After trying out various devices, Cousteau had begun

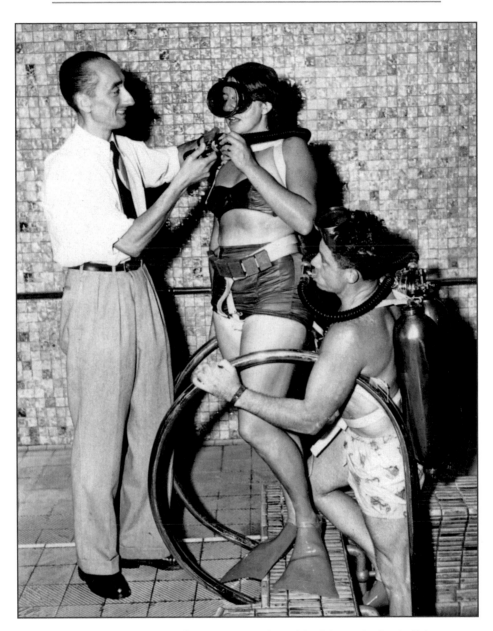

In this 1940s photo, Cousteau works with drivers to test diving equipment in a swimming pool in New York. In 1943, he became the co-inventor, with Émile Gagnan, of the first commercially successful open circuit type of scuba diving equipment, called the Aqua-Lung.

THE UNDERSEA RESEARCH GROUP

Once they had the Aqua-Lung, the Sea Musketeers were eager to further their explorations. With the German occupation of France, however, it wasn't safe to swim just anywhere. Cousteau presented his mission orders to a German admiral, and they were granted permission to explore specific areas in the Mediterranean. Cousteau and his team were particularly interested in exploring sunken ships. The ships that had sunk in the harbor were difficult to get to because the water there was dark and dirty and the currents were too strong.

Finding wrecks farther out was even more challenging because they didn't know the exact locations of the sunken ships. They searched for clues by talking to fishermen, salvage contractors, and other divers. Finally, they spoke with Auguste Marcellin, a leading salvage contractor in Marseilles. After some persuasion, he gave Cousteau and his friends wreck locations with the agreement that he would provide tenders (boats used to bring people and supplies to and from the location) and crews for the dives.

During these dives, Cousteau filmed a new movie, titled *Épaves* ("Shipwreck"). Later, when the German occupation was over,

to wonder about the types of oxygen delivery systems used by pilots who flew at high altitudes. Simone's father, Henri Melchior, was now working for Air Liquide, a company that supplied these devices to pilots. She told her father that Cousteau had given up on trying to perfect oxygen systems, since they were just too dangerous for diving (at any depth), due to the inability to properly control oxygen intake. She explained that he was now looking for a type of equipment known as a dem regulator, which could dispense gas to permit a diver to breathe compressed air from a tank. She explained that

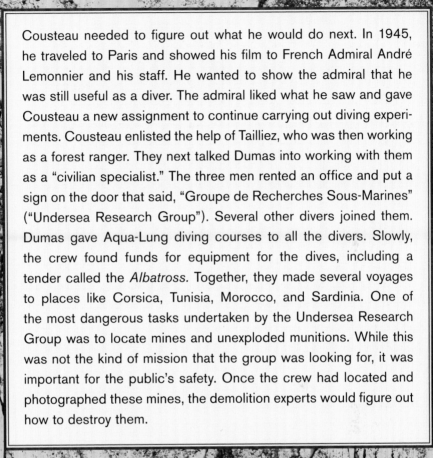

Cousteau needed to figure out what he would do next. In 1945, he traveled to Paris and showed his film to French Admiral André Lemonnier and his staff. He wanted to show the admiral that he was still useful as a diver. The admiral liked what he saw and gave Cousteau a new assignment to continue carrying out diving experiments. Cousteau enlisted the help of Tailliez, who was then working as a forest ranger. They next talked Dumas into working with them as a "civilian specialist." The three men rented an office and put a sign on the door that said, "Groupe de Recherches Sous-Marines" ("Undersea Research Group"). Several other divers joined them. Dumas gave Aqua-Lung diving courses to all the divers. Slowly, the crew found funds for equipment for the dives, including a tender called the *Albatross*. Together, they made several voyages to places like Corsica, Tunisia, Morocco, and Sardinia. One of the most dangerous tasks undertaken by the Undersea Research Group was to locate mines and unexploded munitions. While this was not the kind of mission that the group was looking for, it was important for the public's safety. Once the crew had located and photographed these mines, the demolition experts would figure out how to destroy them.

the air delivery systems used by pilots might be what they were looking for. Melchior listened with interest, and then told her about an engineer at the company who might be able to help. His name was Émile Gagnan.

Cousteau and Gagnan met to discuss what Cousteau was looking for, and whether Gagnan might be able to assist him in designing the device. Gagnan was up for the challenge. Together, they worked on a prototype that would be their first automatic regulator. This system would provide oxygen as needed and also be able to adjust to different amounts of pressure as the diver went deeper underwater. The device would need to be able to adjust to different positions (sideways, upside down, etc.) as the diver changed the angle at which he swam. In addition, the intake device needed to be controlled by the diver, only distributing air when the diver breathed in.

After a first failed attempt, Cousteau and Gagnan figured out that the answer lay in the placement of the exhaust and intake, which would help to keep pressure variations from being disrupted each time the diver changed positions. Up to this point, the systems they had tried often delivered either too much or too little air to the diver each time he or she changed positions and depths. The men realized that the exhaust and intake needed to be in the same plane, or area, in order for the device to work properly. This discovery was the key.

With this problem solved, the next step was to begin filing for patents for this new invention. As it turned out, many other interested parties were working on the same problem and knew about Cousteau and Gagnan's work. It became a race to be the first to get the patent. The possible uses for their device were too many to count. The navy could use it for all kinds of naval missions and for equipment repair. Scientists could use it for underwater research, and divers everywhere could use it in any number of ways. In their patent, Cousteau and Gagnan detailed the assembly of the device, which they called *Scaphandre Autonome* or "Aqua-Lung." Then, they sent their design to a manufacturer and waited for the production to begin.

The Aqua-Lung Arrives

In June 1943, a special package arrived in the mail. Cousteau gathered his wife and close friends, Dumas and Tailliez, to open it. They all knew that Émile Gagnan and Cousteau had been working hard on this device for some time. They hoped that their new device would replace the traditional underwater device, which required a large, brass globe-like structure that covered the head and was tethered to an air supply on the vessel above. For someone like Cousteau, this was far too restrictive. If their design worked, it would revolutionize underwater diving.

Cousteau later compared opening the package with his companions that day to children opening gifts at Christmas. They quickly made a plan for trying out their Aqua-Lung. Everyone had a role to play to make sure Cousteau would be safe once he went underwater. Tailliez and Gagnan readied themselves to dive down to rescue him at a moment's notice. Simone Cousteau floated above the spot where Cousteau went under, watching him through a face mask and breathing through a snorkel as he swam below. Cousteau slowly slipped under the water and began to adjust his breathing and balance. He took his time as he slowly sunk deeper and deeper, watching the bubbles from his exhalations rise to the surface. The sight of these bubbles at the water's surface would come to serve as the all-clear sign to those above that all was well with the diver below.

Finally, when Cousteau got deep enough, he let his body relax and float forward, just like the fish that were swimming all around him. He gently moved the flippers on his feet to glide forward. He looked up to see his wife floating above on the surface of the water. She was a dark silhouette against the bright sunshine that beamed down on the water. He waved at her and she waved back. It worked!

Cousteau began to experiment with movement underwater, paying close attention to how the air delivery system responded with each change. He did somersaults, stood on his head and did other acrobatic stunts. The breathing apparatus continued to work properly. Cousteau and his friends were thrilled. Suddenly, the possibilities of undersea swimming, fishing, and exploring really did seem endless. "From this day forward," Cousteau wrote in *The Silent World,* "we would swim across miles of country no man had known, free and level, with our flesh feeling what the fish scales know."

The Voyages
of *Calypso*

After spending more than a year filming underwater wrecks, submarines, and mine locations, the Sea Musketeers decided that what they really loved was making films, so they shifted their focus in that direction. In 1946, their film *Épaves* (*Shipwreck*) won a special prize at the Cannes Film Festival in Cannes, France. The audience members had never before seen life below the sea and so were astonished by what they saw. Both the Sea Musketeers and Cousteau's family were launched on a whole new path.

With the war over, the Undersea Research Group was going strong. More Aqua-Lungs were being produced, and the group was adding new members. The team knew it was only a matter of time before the news spread about the Aqua-Lung and its capabilities. Unfortunately, the first big news story about their dives reported the death of their friend Maurice Fargues after he set a record depth dive of 385 feet (117 m). Once a diver goes deeper than 140 feet (42.5 m), nitrogen in the body begins to have an effect on the body. The diver acts as though drunk. The senses are dulled, and the ability to think clearly is weakened. This state of mind is called "the rapture of the deep," and it can be life threatening if another diver isn't alongside to provide immediate help in getting the diver back to the surface. This is what happened with Fargues and it illustrated the true dangers of diving. His death was a blow to Cousteau and his team. Nevertheless, Cousteau was someone who always looked

A poster for the 1945 film *Épaves* shows a diver wearing scuba gear and swimming underwater.

to the future and did not dwell on setbacks or tragedy, and so he looked ahead to new endeavors with his team.

SEARCHING FOR TREASURE

The Undersea Research Group decided to head out to its first archaeological expedition off the coast of Tunisia to explore a sunken Roman ship, which was first discovered by Simone Cousteau's grandfather in 1907. Exploring the wreck was a challenge. It took the team longer than expected to find it. By the time they did, they had only one week to explore before they had to leave for another assignment. The ship was 130 feet long and 40 feet wide (39 m by 12 m) and was swarming with fish and debris. In addition, it was all but hidden under all the sand, mud, and other plant life. The divers used a scouring hose to clear the debris from the wreck. The French Film Institute, which had been impressed by Cousteau's first film, had provided him with color film. Once the debris was cleared and settled, Cousteau decided to try out this new film and quietly filmed the divers swimming among the wreck. Often the divers appeared as silhouettes above him, outlined by the sun.

As Cousteau watched through the camera, he imagined what it would be like for someone who'd never been in the ocean, or who had never even swam underwater, to see these sights for the first time. Cousteau himself still marveled at the beauty of this silent world, and his filming made every effort to capture all aspects of undersea diving—the fish, the plants, the light, and the divers swimming quietly among it all. He knew he was doing more than documenting the dive. He was creating a work of art that would show the world the beauty of the sea.

When they were done, the men had salvaged hundreds of ancient artifacts from the wreck, including marble columns more than 2,000 years old. With the exception of a few items, the Undersea Research Group gave all of these artifacts to a museum in Tunisia. Cousteau and his team realized, though, that the Mediterranean, the center of trade for thousands of years, was probably teeming with such wrecks and treasures. Now that divers could reach these depths using the Aqua-Lung, the potential for more great discoveries was overwhelming.

Demand for the Aqua-Lung Grows

In the four years after the formation of the Undersea Research Group, their resources grew and grew. They went from occupying one small office to taking over a three-story building, which included a machine shop, photo and chemistry labs, and a drafting room. In addition, they added several diving tenders to their fleet. The building even included living space for the crew. By this time, demand for the Aqua-Lung was growing in both Europe and the United States. This was in large part thanks to a 1948 article in *Scientific Illustrated* by James Dugan. In the article, Dugan described the film footage he'd seen of Cousteau's dive, as well as an interview with Cousteau, which lasted several hours. In addition, the U.S. Navy purchased Aqua-Lungs for their experimental diving team. It didn't take long for demand for Aqua-Lungs to outstrip the supply. Cousteau soon realized that he and the Undersea Research Group were making a difference when it came to the world and its understanding of the sea. The more people who wanted to experience it, he knew, the more people would care about its preservation.

THE BATHYSCAPHE

At about this time, Auguste Piccard, an inventor and explorer from Switzerland, approached the group about creating a diving machine. Piccard had experimented with a gondola type mechanism he used as an air balloon that could reach extremely high altitudes. Now he wanted to try a similar vehicle to go far below the sea. Piccard called his invention a bathyscaphe. The plan was to have one man inside the bathyscaphe, which had a mechanical claw for grasping specimens. It also had harpoon cannons for spearing fish and, finally, a glass porthole, through which the person inside could film the undersea world outside. This was the sort of invention that Cousteau relished. Any sort of device that could be used to dive deeper and explore more of the sea was a promising and worthwhile endeavor.

Cousteau hoped to be the first to travel in the bathyscaphe's first dive but, unfortunately, he broke his foot while playing tennis with his son Jean-Michel. In addition, some of Cousteau's team and their families were wary of sending a loved one on this trial run because Piccard had the reputation of being a daredevil who didn't make safety much of a priority. This mission in particular seemed to be an extremely dangerous venture. At the same time, if it was successful, the diver who went down would get all the glory. Cousteau and Piccard decided it was worth the risk. This would be the deepest dive man had ever witnessed—five times deeper than any had gone before.

On October 1, 1948, they set sail for the coast of West Africa to make their first test dive. The bathyscaphe looked like a miniature

Professor Auguste Piccard is seen wearing a life jacket as he emerges from the conning tower of the bathyscaphe *Trieste* after making a world-record dive of 10,335 feet (3,150 m) from Pinza Island, off the west coast of Italy.

dirigible. Cousteau and his men drew straws to see who would get to go on the first dive, a ritual they performed for all their dives. Théodore Monod, director of the Institute for Black Africa, won the draw. Then Monod and Piccard climbed in, and the opening was sealed and the sphere was lowered into the sea. Divers accompanied it partway down to see that all was well. The sphere was lowered to 200 feet (61 m). Five hours later, the sphere surfaced and the crew cheered at the successful completion of this first dive. However, for the following test, the sphere was set to dive 4,600 feet (1,402 m), unmanned. During that test, the bathyscape was damaged and the crew was unable to complete its goal. While this dive was considered a failure, the experiment and the publicity it generated established Cousteau and his team as top ocean explorers.

THAT'S *LIFE*

In 1950, Cousteau met a woman named Perry Miller, a United Nations cultural attaché who was looking for new documentary films about postwar Europe. Cousteau's father, who now was working as his son's business manager, heard about Miller and showed her Cousteau's first films. Miller was impressed. She presented the films at a party in New York, where an editor from *Life* magazine was captivated by them. In November, *Life* ran a story showcasing images from Cousteau's films. At that time, the magazine had a circulation of over 10 million subscribers, plus more readers who bought the magazine from newsstands. Just one day after the Cousteau issue came out, Miller received a call from Universal Pictures, the Hollywood studio. Universal wanted to discuss who had the rights to the films. She put him in touch with Cousteau's business manager who sold the exclusive rights to the company for $11,000.

FINDING *CALYPSO*

With all of their success, Cousteau and his crew felt energized and were ready to do more. They decided that they needed a new ship that could hold more cargo and crew—something which would allow the crew to travel for months at a time. However, the French Navy was not quite ready to fund such a vessel. Cousteau was told by his admiral to keep working for advancement in the navy and become an admiral himself. That way, he could get his own ship. Cousteau, however, wanted to take another route. The navy's recommendation would take too long to achieve, and he wanted his own ship now! He requested three months furlough time to, in his words, "look after personal affairs."

Although banks were lending to many businesses to help rebuild France after World War II, they were reluctant to lend money to Cousteau for building a ship of his own design. He approached friends and business connections to try to raise the money, but he still wasn't able to raise enough to build the ship he wanted. Finally, the Cousteaus contacted some old friends whom they'd known during the war. These friends introduced Cousteau to a wealthy lawyer named Loel Guinness. Guinness was keen on the idea of using a research ship to film ocean exploration. He thought such a venture could change the world. Rather than build a new ship, he suggested finding a ship that already existed. At the time, many ships were being sold as war surplus. Why not find one of these and then retrofit it to accommodate Cousteau's needs?

In 1951, Cousteau found what he was looking for. It was a 66-foot Royal Navy minesweeper used in World War II. The boat was christened as *Calypso* in 1941. (Its name was inspired by the Greek nymph who held Ulysses captive on the island of Gozo for 10 years.) By the time Cousteau found the ship, it had been converted to a ferry. Guinness bought the ship on July 19, 1950, and became its official owner. In turn, he leased it to Cousteau for a token payment of one franc (about one U.S. dollar at the time) per year in perpetuity on only two conditions: first, that Cousteau must never tell who paid for the boat, and second, that he could never ask Guinness for another dime. Cousteau agreed to this generous offer at once.

Back in Toulon, Cousteau requested that the navy extend his furlough to three years, agreeing to return to duty in case of war. The furlough was granted. Cousteau tried to convince his old friend Tailliez to join him, but Tailliez decided to stay with the Undersea Research Group. Dumas, however, was eager to join Cousteau.

Calypso is pictured in this still from Cousteau's 1956 documentary *The Silent World.*

His wife and children would also join Simone and the Cousteau children aboard the ship.

Despite the generous funding by Guinness, Cousteau knew that he would need more money to help run the ship, feed the crew, and pay for gas and equipment. He planned to make films and write books about his explorations to raise money, but a friend who knew finances warned him that the sales from these products—even the sales from the increasingly popular Aqua-Lung—would not be enough to sustain the ship and crew. He suggested that Cousteau set up a nonprofit corporation. While the corporation could receive revenue from the sales of its movies, books, and other materials, its nonprofit status would allow investors, grants, science organizations, and private companies to donate money to its cause. This seemed to be the best approach, so Cousteau founded the Campagnes Océanographiques Françaises (French Oceanographic Campaigns). Cousteau brought *Calypso* to Antibes, France, and began her transformation.

Calypso Sets Sail

In June 1951, *Calypso* began her first sea trials. The crew consisted of the Cousteau family and a few friends. At the time, Jean-Michel was 13 and Philippe was 11 and served on the crew as cabin boys. Simone Cousteau was in charge of stewardship.

On November 24, 1951, *Calypso* set sail on the Red Sea, where Cousteau would shoot the first underwater film in color at 150 feet

A FULLY-LOADED VESSEL

Under Cousteau's supervision, *Calypso* was transformed from a minesweeper to a fully-equipped research vessel. Additions to the ship included:

- An underwater observation chamber on the prow—with eight portholes that allowed people to view underwater life
- A special tube attached to the bottom of the ship that divers could use to exit the ship underwater
- A crow's nest
- A towing winch for pulling up artifacts and dredges
- A compression chamber
- A machine shop for repairing equipment
- Several cabins for the crew

Calypso sailed for more than 40 years. It served as a vessel, an operations base, and a home. It sailed the Indian Ocean and Antarctica. It sailed up the Mississippi and Amazon Rivers. It survived breakdowns, hurricanes, storms, ice, and sandbanks. Most importantly, it became a symbol of hope for ocean exploration, research, and preservation.

(45.5 meters) deep. Other members of the crew included François Saout as captain, Octave Leandri (nicknamed "Titi") as engineer, René Montupet as chief mechanic, Jean Beltran as first mate, Fernand Hanen as cook, and Jacques Ertaud and Jean de Wouters d'Oplinter as photographers. Cousteau's old friend Dumas was diving supervisor. There were also scientists, photographers, and a ship's doctor, whom Simone also assisted. Even so, all the crew took turns doing various jobs, depending on the needs of the crew and ship.

In addition to exploring sea life, Cousteau knew that a key discovery—and one that could be very lucrative—would be to find evidence of oil. On their first trip to Crete, Cousteau and his crew were merry and optimistic, but perhaps a little nervous, too. Would this expensive ship help them discover enough interesting specimens and evidence of oil to help garner the interest of the donors they needed to keep them going? The answer was yes. Using echo sounders, the geologists on board found evidence of oil-bearing shale. Divers took samples of water from different depths to give hydrologists evidence of the complexity of seawater. Using nets and spear guns, other divers caught hundreds of sea creatures and plant life, which they bottled for study. Many of these specimens had never been seen before. In addition to gathering these valuable samples, Cousteau and the filmmakers and photographers used color film to take hundreds of underwater images of the sea and its creatures that no one but a small number of divers had ever seen before.

This topographic and photographic documentation was the first of its kind. Cousteau knew that the only way for people to really understand the sea was for them to see it for themselves. Since this was impossible for the vast majority of scientists and other people who would be interested, Cousteau became their link.

Back in Toulon, Cousteau received a letter from the American writer who'd helped launch Cousteau's celebrity in *Life* magazine, James Dugan. He had heard about Cousteau's latest endeavors and wanted to get involved. He thought Cousteau's adventures, accompanied by photographs, would make a popular book. Even though

Cousteau was more interested in making a full-length film, he realized that Dugan was probably right. A book with photographs illustrating the French Oceanographic Campaigns could bring a whole new level of public awareness to their group—as well as funding. Dugan got to work as the book's ghostwriter.

THE SEARCH FOR MORE TREASURE

At about the same time, Cousteau approached the National Geographic Society about helping to fund a new expedition that would involve taking a submarine to far greater depths than divers could with their Aqua-Lungs. He insisted that such a project could help educate the world about its most precious resource, the oceans. The U.S. broadcasting network CBS had also begun to show interest in featuring Cousteau's footage in their documentary series *Omnibus*. However, neither organization had signed any contracts, and Cousteau needed money. The team began to

AN UNLIKELY ICON

As *Calypso's* fame grew over the years, the boat has been the inspiration for many artists. For example, singer/songwriter John Denver wrote the song "Calypso" in 1975 as a tribute to Cousteau, his crew, and the ship. It reached number one on the Billboard Hot 100 chart. Voice-over actor Tom Kenny's role as the French Narrator in the popular television series *SpongeBob SquarePants* was inspired by Cousteau. *The Life Aquatic with Steve Zissou*, a 2004 film directed by Wes Anderson, is an homage to Cousteau. The movie stars actors Bill Murray (as Steve Zissou), Cate Blanchett, Owen Wilson, and Anjelica Houston.

explore the possibility of carrying out salvage missions to raise funds for their projects.

Dumas and Cousteau learned from their friend Gaston Christianini of a recent salvage project in the islet of Grand Congloué in the Marseilles basin. The friend had been collecting scrap metal, but when he described the wreckage area, Cousteau and Dumas sensed that the wreck area may include something more significant than metal. Cousteau and Dumas took a small group to the site, including Fernand Benoît, the director of antiquities of Provence, in case they needed an expert to identify their findings. Cousteau was the first to explore the site. At about 100 feet (30.5 m) down, he realized he was swimming over a discovery much greater than they'd imagined—a very large shipwreck, complete with cargo. Buried under debris, Cousteau drew out a chalice. He showed the cup to Benoît, who estimated that it must have been as old as the second century B.C.

Cousteau and Dumas realized they had a major discovery on their hands. They quickly contacted the Borely Museum in the city of Marseille and *National Geographic* to get funding for the excavation. For the next year, they worked on developing equipment and gathering a crew of scientists specifically for an archaeological dig. Back at the site, Cousteau and his professional divers used an underwater TV camera for the first time, taking it down to a depth of 150 feet (45.5 m) to film the wreck while the archaeologists, who didn't know how to dive, watched the broadcast of the images captured by the camera on a screen aboard *Calypso*. The scientists instructed the divers on where to search and where not to. The crew brought back thousands of amphorae (Greek or Roman jars), pottery shards, and other artifacts, which were taken to the Borely Museum and the Roman Docks of Marseille.

Revealing the Silent World

I took James Dugan about a year to help Cousteau write *The Silent World: A Story of Undersea Discovery and Adventure, by the First Men to Swim at Record Depths with the Freedom of Fish*. It was published in February 1953 and, one month later, hit the *New York Times* bestseller list. In this book, Cousteau and Dumas describe what it was like to become "menfish" and swim underwater with all kinds of sea life, including sharks and octopuses. They described the ancient Mediterranean shipwrecks and underwater caves they'd explored, detailing the conversations, the thrills, and setbacks they'd experienced. What was most significant about the book and their adventures was that they were the first to use the Aqua-Lung for such expeditions. The book describes in detail how they created and developed the Aqua-Lung and their desire to popularize diving. At the time of the book's publication, they were early explorers of a new world. They would go on to capture most of their adventures on film and share them with millions of people in the follow-up film of the same name. *The Silent World* was the first book to document this type of underwater adventure and it caused a sensation. The year the book was published, it sold more than 5 million copies around the world.

Earlier in that year, another book about the sea was also published. *The Sea Around Us* by Rachel Carson described the fragile condition of the Earth's waters. Carson warned readers that humanity must start to treat the sea with care and stop polluting it. This book won the National Book Award. When Carson read Cousteau's book, she recognized him as an ally in the quest to save the Earth's waters. She understood that Cousteau's fame also made him a fellow advocate of the sea. The more Cousteau learned about the sea, the more he was becoming its greatest conservationist and spokesperson.

After spending several months prospecting oil to raise money, Cousteau and the French Oceanographic Campaigns were ready for a new adventure. They had finally received a grant from the French Ministry of National Education, with the agreement that a group of marine biologists, appointed by the National Center for Scientific Research, would accompany Cousteau on his next trip. *Calypso* was now officially known as the French National Oceanographic Research ship.

FILMING *THE SILENT WORLD*

In March 1953, the crew prepared to set sail on a four-month long expedition to shoot the movie version of *The Silent World*. Before setting off, Cousteau, Dumas, and Louis Malle, a new photographer who joined their team, made improvements on their cameras for undersea photography. Filming underwater became more challenging the deeper they dove because of the lack of light. By 1948, Cousteau had been using lights that were linked to the surface with an electric cable or tether, a technique he used to film his first color footage of underwater sea life. Cousteau and his team continued to study light underwater so that they could perfect the use of film to get the best results. By 1955, they had rebuilt their cameras with new lenses, drives, and more airtight and maneuverable housings.

In this scene from *The Silent World*, filmed 1954 to 1955, Cousteau drives an underwater electric scooter, while another diver holds on to a sea turtle.

For their still cameras, they added the same strobes and floodlights with which they had outfitted their movie cameras.

Their route would take them from the Red Sea to the Seychelles Islands in the Indian Ocean. From there, they'd travel to Madagascar off the coast of Africa. The crew numbered 25. Just before they set sail, *National Geographic* contacted Cousteau and offered him a grant for an illustrated story of their travels, which would use Cousteau's name for the byline. Cousteau agreed to this. The magazine also sent Luis Marden, a photographer, to record the expedition both underwater and aboard *Calypso*. Marden would take more than 1,200 photographs, the biggest collection of underwater color photos ever taken up to that time.

THE SILENT WORLD DEBUTS

Three years after the publication of *The Silent World,* the compan-ion film of the same title was released. Readers who were fascinated by the book couldn't wait to see the movie featuring the sea life they'd read about. In the film, Cousteau and his co-director, Malle, created a documentary not just about sea life, but also about what it was like to dive among it—to swim to depths that are dangerous to the human body. In his narration, Cousteau dramatically describes what it's like to swim to depths where light fades to black and water temperatures plummet. He describes the rapture of the deep and how the human body is quickly affected by the pressure at 140 feet

WHALES BREAK THE SILENCE

One day, while sailing off the coast of Kenya, *Calypso* encountered a pod of whales. Before they could move out of the way in time, the boat hit one of the whales. Badly injured, the whale was obviously suffering. Two other whales came to its aid, one on either side to hold it up, but then, another tragedy struck. A baby whale struck the ship's propeller and suffered horrible deep gashes on its body. The echo sounder on the ship captured the whales' mournful cries. Suddenly, the whales reformed their pod and swam away. Almost immediately, a team of sharks arrived, smelling the blood the whales left behind.

Later, when Cousteau was writing about the scene in the ship's logs, he noted that he was sure the whales were communicating with one another, both at the time of the collision and before they fled from the sharks. Horrific as the scene was, Cousteau's cam-era team filmed what they could. Later, scientists would study this footage, which also further inspired the study of whales and their unique method of communication.

A driver observes fish from the unique vantage point deep under the sea in this scene from *The Silent World*. The 1956 film gave viewers a chance to see a world many could only imagine.

(42.5 m) and deeper where the nitrogen in the human body begins to alter a person's sense of balance and ability to think straight. The film also captures the divers as they resurface from the silent world back onto the deck of *Calypso*. Here, the divers have trouble walking in their fins while carrying their heavy tanks, no longer the graceful swimmers that were shown moments before.

The film also shows the divers swimming with dazzling sea creatures, as well as exploring sunken shipwrecks. In one of the most memorable scenes, a group of dolphins swims alongside *Calypso*, staying with it as it both speeds up and slows down, sometimes even stopping to wait for the boat catch up. Yet the film also portrays the difficult scenes of the sea, such as when a team of sharks feeds on an injured baby whale. This particular scene is followed by one where the crew captures the sharks and cuts them up on deck.

The film was more successful than anyone involved with making it could have hoped for. It won the prestigious Palme d'Or at the Cannes Film Festival. Later, in 1956, it won an Academy Award in the United States for best documentary film. The more people saw Cousteau's films, the more they wanted to explore the silent world themselves. Sales of Aqua-Lungs boomed both in the United States and Europe.

Among the film's admirers was Prince Rainier of Monaco who offered Cousteau the position of director of the Oceanographic Museum in Monte Carlo. The museum was the oldest undersea museum and research center. Rainier believed that by employing Cousteau's fame, he could draw much funding and many research scientists to the museum. Cousteau accepted the position and finally officially resigned from the French Navy.

THE DIVING SAUCER

During the now-famous excavation at Grand Gongloué, Cousteau was constantly thinking about ways to improve how archeological objects were filmed and removed. He thought back to the bathyscaphe experiment and wondered if a similar vehicle could be used. Finally, he got an idea. He took a saucer from the table and placed it right side up. Then, he took another and put it face down on top. That was it: a lightweight saucer-shaped cabin that could be lowered from *Calypso* into the sea. It would be a new underwater vehicle designed specifically for scientific exploration.

It took five more years (from 1953 to 1958) to make Cousteau's idea a reality. During this time, Cousteau, along with engineer Jean Mollard and André Laban developed the SP-350, which they called *Hull Number One*. The yellow metal submarine was 5 feet high and 6 feet 7 inches across (1.5 by 2.04 m). It weighed 3.5 tons (3.18 metric tons). The men thought it still looked just like the two saucers Cousteau had put together as an example of his idea five years before. Unlike the bathyscaphe, *Hull Number One* would be able

(continues on page 62)

TIME MAGAZINE

In 1959, Cousteau was invited to go to New York to address the World Oceanic Congress. One thousand scientists and explorers from all over the world attended to discuss the future of the world's oceans. They discussed the new relationship between humans and the sea, and how new technology was allowing humans to use the sea's resources in promising new ways for oil and industry in particular. What was once considered an endless resource was being seen more clearly as a precious one. When Cousteau spoke, he gave one small but powerful example of how industry and development was impacting the sea. He described how a recent landfill development off the coast of Monaco had had a devastating impact on marine organisms, and went on to describe how this destruction then affected fish and other sea life. He also described the serious threat that nuclear energy plants slated for development would have on the sea. He described the dangers of dumping radioactive waste onto the shorelines of the Mediterranean and the profound effect this would have on sea life and fishing. This moment was a huge turning point for Cousteau and his journey toward becoming a conservationist. He realized that his films and books could influence how the world treated the sea and its resources, both in terms of developing a greater appreciation for the Earth, and of inspiring people to take action and behave more responsibly. He came to believe that the more he educated people about the sea, the better he could help save it.

After the meeting, Cousteau and his crew sailed *Calypso* to the Oceanographic Institution on Nantucket Sound. Everywhere he went, he met people who had been captivated by *The Silent World*.

A reporter and photographer for *Time* magazine interviewed him onboard and the story became the lead feature in the March 28, 1960 issue, with Cousteau featured on the cover.

Cousteau and his wife, Simone, pose with their pet dachshund aboard *Calypso* on August 30, 1959.

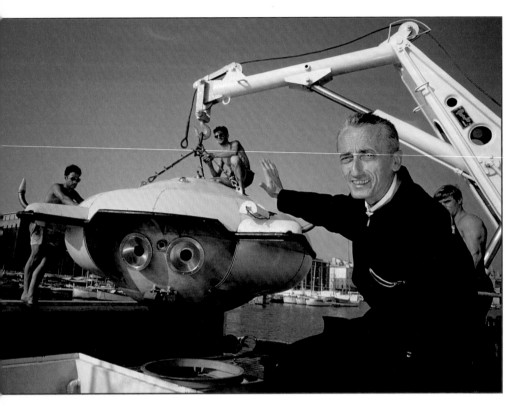

Cousteau gestures toward his bathyscaphe in Puerto Rico in January 1960.

(continued from page 59)

to carry two members who would be able to control its movements as they lay on their bellies and peered out through Plexiglas ports.

Before they could try it out with crew, *Hull Number One* needed to be tested. After it was loaded on board *Calypso,* it was attached to a long cable and lowered into the water to a depth of 2,000 feet (609.5 m). All seemed to be going well, but when they tried to haul it back up, the cable snapped and *Hull Number One* sank to the bottom of the sea, over 3,000 feet (914.5 m) below. Using special sonar equipment, the crew could tell that *Hull Number One* had stayed intact, but it would be costly and difficult to recover. Thus, the engineers got to work on *Hull Number Two,* which they later nicknamed *La Soucoupe Plongeante* ("The Diving Saucer") both because it looked like the flying saucers portrayed in science fiction films, and because of how it resembled Cousteau's original idea of putting two saucers together.

Better Luck the Second Time

La Soucoupe Plongeante was an improvement over *Hull Number One*. Twin propulsion jets were added to the bow, which drew water in and squirted it back out through two tubes. These could be swiveled on command using the controls inside, and they allowed the craft to have a full range of motion. With these jets, the saucer could move at a speed of about 2 knots (3.7 kilometers per hour). Its unique seating arrangement allowed two people to stretch out on mattresses and look out through portholes. These portholes allowed them to get very close to their subjects for filming. Once again, diving deep meant they had to figure out how to light up the darkness they would encounter. Three movable lights were attached to the saucer at different angles. These lights allowed the scientists to see objects up to 33 feet (10 m) away. For filming, they used an Edgerton stroboscopic camera, which was invented by Harold Edgerton. They also used a movie camera with a floodlight. Three sonar transducers were also added to the vessel that could transmit signals to a screen on the instrument panel to help the two crew members navigate. The diving saucer also had a radio and a tape recorder onboard, and a sampling arm that allowed it to grasp objects. The arm was controlled from inside the cabin. There was enough oxygen in the breathing system to provide the crew with up to 24 hours worth of air, even though the ship was intended to stay underwater for only 4 to 5 hours per dive.

Once the saucer was ready for its first dive, Cousteau decided that it would be best to test it in relatively shallow water so that it would be easier to retrieve if anything went wrong. The first test took place in the Caribbean, off the continental shelf of Puerto Rico, where the water was about 80 feet (24 m) deep. The saucer was attached to *Calypso* with a winch cable. After just a few test dives, the group began to get very excited. The saucer was easy to maneuver, the visibility through the ports was very clear, and it moved fast through the water.

Finally, it was time for the real test. The cable was detached, and the saucer dove down to 200 feet (61 m). With his camera, Cousteau swam alongside the bright yellow craft as deep as he could to capture the action. He wrote instructions to the crew on a white dinner plate with a grease pencil and held them up to the porthole. He instructed them to spin, do a lazy eight, and practice emergency ascents to the surface. Each of these maneuvers was successful. After a few mishaps with figuring out which type of battery to use for the deeper depths, the diving saucer was considered ready to go.

The team spent the following year making several dives in the Mediterranean Sea. For each dive, they needed one experienced controller, but also allowed scientists to go along. As a result, for the first time, geologists and biologists were able to see firsthand depths of the ocean that they'd never seen before. Using the claw, they could collect hundreds of samples for study, such as rocks, mud, sea creatures, plants, and many other objects.

La Soucoupe Plongeante participated in more than 1,500 dives in its lifetime. It was the first scientific submersible and its development led to a whole new era of underwater research.

Living Under the Sea

Jacques Cousteau and his crew returned to Marseilles at the end of 1960. The new diving saucer was a huge success. Cousteau believed that it was only a matter of time before scientists discovered a way to live below the sea for short stretches of time—or longer. Cousteau wasn't the only one with a vision of undersea living, however. At about the same time, George Bond, a commander in the U. S. Navy, had been trying to convince the navy of the usefulness of underwater shelters—structures that could house divers for many days or even weeks.

One of the complications that people face when they stay deep underwater for a long time is the rise of nitrogen levels in their blood and tissues. This means that the process of sending divers down into the depths and then returning them to the surface needs to take place gradually. A diver who descends or rises too quickly may experience decompression sickness. This can be extremely dangerous and even deadly. However, Bond thought that divers who stayed below long enough would eventually become accustomed to the nitrogen levels. Therefore, they would be able to work on underwater construction projects for both the U.S. Navy and private businesses, such as underwater pipelines for offshore oil rigs.

Although the navy didn't show much interest in Bond's ideas, he didn't want to give up. He was sure he was onto something that could revolutionize undersea construction—maybe even how people lived on Earth. After seeing *The Silent World,* he figured that if anyone would be interested in such a venture, it would be Jacques Cousteau. Bond was right. Cousteau had been ruminating about this very subject himself for years.

CONSHELF I

Cousteau and Bond got to work on the first phase of the project they called Continental Shelf I, or Conshelf I for short. Conshelf I was a watertight steel cylinder 18 feet long and 8 feet wide (5.5 by 2.5 m), big enough to hold two divers. Nicknamed "Diogenes," the cylinder would need to be anchored with chains to a depth of 37 feet (11 m). It was hoped that the two divers could swim for up to five hours every day, and then return to the cylinder. They could swim up to depths of 80 feet (24 m), but never above the 37 feet (11 m) mark where the cylinder hovered. The cylinder also had a hole on the bottom big enough for the divers to fit through. Seawater was kept out of the cylinder by the air pressure inside. Divers Albert Falco and Claude Wesly were selected to take part in the experiment. They were dubbed "aquanauts."

On September 14, 1962, *Calypso* towed Diogenes to the abandoned island of Frioul, located about 2.5 miles (4 km) from Marseille. The cylinder was also equipped with cameras inside to monitor and record the event. Everyone wondered if the men would be able to handle living in their tiny new home for an entire week. Even though the two divers had been involved in building Diogenes from the beginning, everything felt different to them once they took up residence underwater. The small space contained two berths, a small bookcase, a radio and a television for broadcasting the French national broadcasting station. There was also a table with two chairs and a place to prepare food. Food would be lowered down to them from *Calypso* by pressure cookers. They even had a shower with hot water, which was piped down to them from *Calypso*. The only obvious missing utility was a toilet. The men would have go to the bathroom in the ocean outside.

Living Underwater

It took about five hours for both men's bodies to become saturated with nitrogen. This meant that before they could resurface, they'd need to go through a process called reoxygenation. Two doctors dove down to the cylinder twice a day to examine them. These exams lasted two and a half hours each. The doctors took blood tests and measured the men's heart rates and blood pressure.

For the first two days, all seemed to be going well. Falco and Wesly enjoyed playing to the cameras, both to those located inside Diogenes and to those carried by the cameramen who filmed them as they swam outside their miniature home. On the third day, however, it was clear to those observing them that something was wrong. The first visiting divers to actually enter Diogenes found Falco and Wesly in a forlorn state. They complained of nightmares and fears of equipment failure. Cousteau became deeply concerned. The next day, he sent down a psychologist to examine them. The doctor couldn't find anything physically wrong with the men, but noted that they suffered from extreme stress from being monitored and interviewed constantly, in addition to having to live in such a small space. The process was having an effect on the men's spirits. Cousteau limited the doctors' visits to once a day, and instructed the others to give Falco and Wesly more space. Slowly, the men's spirits seemed to improve.

Finally, when it was time for the men to resurface, Cousteau knew they needed to take things slowly and carefully. The men needed time to safely rebalance the oxygen levels in their blood before they could come back up. When Falco and Wesly finally reached the surface, they were thrilled to see blue sky, sun, and land again, but they were also both excited by new dreams of future undersea colonies and the seemingly endless promise of living underwater. They believed that providing a bigger living space and involving more people to keep each other company would lead to a new and revolutionary way to live. They weren't the only ones.

A month after he returned with Diogenes to Marseilles, Cousteau traveled to London and spoke in front of the World Congress on Underwater Activities. He discussed how the experiment with Conshelf I might contribute to underwater oil and mineral development. Operating such huge endeavors required divers who could anchor and maintain drilling rigs, pumps, and pipelines. What had once seemed a complicated, extremely dangerous, and impossible operation suddenly seemed to be a possible venture, where teams of workers might live and work below the water's surface for days, or even weeks, at a time.

Cousteau also told his audience that he believed a new species was evolving, which he called *Homo aquaticus.* He even stated that it might be possible to surgically implant human beings with gills to allow them to extract oxygen from water so they could breathe. The delegates seemed a bit stunned at first, and then almost amused, though their respect for Cousteau caused them to muffle their surprised reaction to his proposals. A few of them worried that Cousteau was losing his mind because of his belief in such farfetched ideas that seemed the stuff of science fiction. Cousteau, however, insisted that these ideas weren't so farfetched. He referred them to Jules Verne's *20,000 Leagues Under the Sea:* If Verne's visions could come true, why couldn't Cousteau's?

CONSHELF II

In 1963, Cousteau and his team had drawn enough interest and funding to build Conshelf II, this time locating it in the Red Sea. Columbia Pictures, the Hollywood movie studio, put up half the money to make a film about the reefs on the Red Sea, as well as the divers who would be living in Conshelf II. The other investor was a French petroleum consortium. Cousteau's old friend and inventor of the Edgerton stroboscopic camera, Harold Edgerton (who was known by the nickname "Papa Flash"), had also invented a seismic transceiver that was able to detect hard objects buried in sediment up to several feet thick. It could also sample the chemistry of seawater to detect petroleum levels, which would make it useful for discovering possible oil sources. This part of the project greatly interested the French petroleum consortium.

Conshelf II was a far more ambitious project than Conshelf I. Designed like a small village, it was built on the floor of the Red Sea, 27 miles (43.45 km) north of Port Sudan, in the middle of one of the greatest known coral reefs in the world. The structure was anchored at a depth of 33 feet (10 m). The main house was called Starfish House. It was designed as a central hub with five rooms that stretched from its center like arms. A chamber that was called

Conshelf II sits at the bottom of Sudan's Shab Rumi reef in the Red Sea.

The Cousteaus and their crew relax in their submersible after a day of work in 1963.

a "moonpool" was built at the bottom of the hub through which the inhabitants could leave Starfish House to enter the sea.

The diving saucer would play a crucial role in both filming and delivering most of the supplies. To "park" it, they built a steel garage located 50 feet (15 m) from Starfish House.

The Starfish House's residents lived well. They were fed top-restaurant quality food. They had a television, a radio, and even a telephone to help them communicate and feel connected to the world above. The house also had large picture windows that looked out on the undersea world. Air was pumped into the house through a pipe that ran to the surface. In addition to the men, this Conshelf had a new inhabitant: Esly's pet parrot.

TV cameras in every room monitored the men's activities. Conshelf II was like a movie set, but the inhabitants were able to find some privacy whenever they needed it. This was a key to their mental health as they'd learned from the first Conshelf experiment.

To film underwater, Cousteau used lights that were attached to very long cables from above and several cameras. He used what was called an "owl eye" to film in low light. The owl eye allowed him to capture nautiluses (a type of mollusk) on film for the first time.

They also installed a station they called "Deep Cabin" 50 feet (15 m) below Starfish House. This was a smaller, two-person station. Like the first Conshelf, Deep Cabin was far more challenging to live in, both because it had room for only two occupants and had far fewer amenities. Deep Cabin's occupants also faced the challenges of colder temperatures and more difficulty with breathing. To compensate,

WORLD WITHOUT SUN

After the success of Conshelf II, Cousteau assembled all the footage they'd shot to produce his second major documentary, *World Without Sun*. Filming *The Silent World* had taught the filmmakers the key ingredients to a successful undersea documentary: the right balance of information, adventure, and excitement. Audiences had been fascinated by the problems that divers faced in regard to breathing and water pressure, in addition to the effects of underwater living on the human body. Starfish House offered plenty of entertainment and fascination as it inspired the idea that living undersea might really be possible for human beings. Watching the diving saucer zip around like a modern car provided something like a glimpse into the future. The drama that played out in Deep Cabin provided plenty of suspense as the men struggled with the heat and the unfamiliar mixture of helium and oxygen they were required to breathe at such a depth. The elements made for an exciting and informative film. In December 1964, the film was released to an eager audience, and Cousteau won his second Oscar for best documentary.

Deep Cabin's occupants were limited to just one-week stays, while the occupants of Starfish House had to stay for one month.

Starfish House's residents had a marvelous time. When Simone Cousteau, curious about Starfish House living and tired of the relentless heat she experienced onboard *Calypso,* dove down for a visit, she loved it so much, she decided to stay for the rest of the experiment. She and her husband even celebrated their 26th wedding anniversary there.

Conshelf II was a great success. The team had proved that it really was possible for human beings to live under the sea for weeks at a time. Petroleum engineers were particularly interested because it demonstrated how divers could work underwater on long-term, off-shore drilling projects. By then, several vast pools of oil had been discovered in the Gulf of Mexico, the Persian Gulf, and off the California coast, and the idea of building underwater chambers for workers to stay in while they maintained the equipment seemed ideal. However, these projects would require divers to work at a depth of 300 feet (91.5 m) or deeper, much deeper than Conshelf II. This challenge spurred the construction of Conshelf III.

CONSHELF III

By 1965, the construction of Conshelf III was complete. The 20-foot-long (6.1 m) steel sphere was painted a bright yellow and black. *Calypso* towed the sphere from a dock at Monte Carlo to an area off Cape Ferrat on the east coast of Monaco, outside Nice, France. Six men were prepared for the pressurization needed to live in an even greater depth underwater. When they were ready, they entered the sphere, which was lowered to 325 feet (99 m) below the surface. This time, they would live below the sea for 27 days. On board was a commander (André Laban), a doctor (Oceanographic Museum physicist Jacques Roillet), three working divers (Christian Bownia, Raymond Coll, and Yves Omer), and a cameraman (Jacques Cousteau's son, Philippe Cousteau).

Conshelf III had a different layout from the first two Conshelf structures. This sphere had two floors. The bottom floor contained

In this October 1965 image, divers prepare for a test dive in Conshelf III, which was deposited into the Mediterranean Sea, off the coast of Monaco.

sleeping quarters, the toilet, and storage. The upper floor had a kitchen, food pantry, galley, and communications station.

In order to be able to live at this depth, where the pressure was greater, the men had to breathe an unusual mixture of oxygen and helium. This also served as an experiment to see how this mixture would affect them. Unfortunately, the effects were not very pleasant. It caused the men to lose their sense of taste, and some of their other senses, including smell, were dulled significantly. Breathing helium also made them speak in high-pitched voices that made them difficult to understand. However, the men carried on, performing tasks that simulated what underwater workers would have to endure while working on oil machinery.

The men lived in Conshelf III together for three weeks. Each day, they worked on a mock oil well while their capabilities to work underwater were evaluated. The experiment showed once again that humans could live undersea for long periods of time, this time, at even greater depths.

When it was time to resurface, it took two days to prepare the men's bodies to adjust to surface conditions. The experiment had drawn so much attention (also with the help of Cousteau's many contacts at news outlets), that 17 television stations from around Europe provided live broadcast coverage of the men's return.

The Undersea World of Jacques Cousteau

As he did with Conshelf II, Cousteau wanted to produce a film about Conshelf III. During the three weeks, he filmed Conshelf III

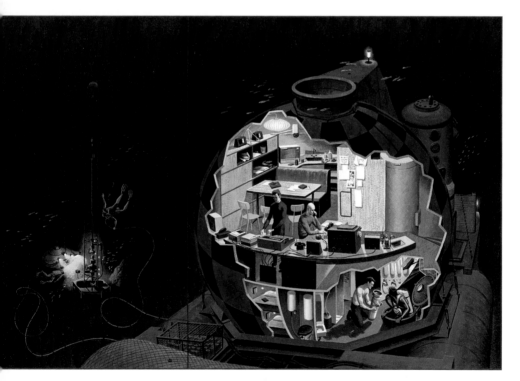

An artist's rendering shows the interior of Conshelf III, inhabited by scientists and divers in 1965.

SEA FLEAS

In addition to the diving saucer, two single-passenger subs, or scooters, nicknamed "Sea Fleas," were brought aboard *Calypso*. These tiny subs (6.5 x 10 feet, or 1.9 x 3 m) could dive up to 1,000 feet (350 m) below the surface. Cousteau described the small machines as lawnmowers with propellers. They were very easy to maneuver and could travel for about one hour at a time. Similar to the SP-350 diving saucer, the Sea Fleas were built by the aeronautical factory Sud-Aviation. The pilot controlled them with a joystick with buttons on each finger of the grip. The Sea Fleas worked together as a team. The pilots were able to see each other through Plexiglas portholes and could take turns filming each other doing various tasks. Each vehicle had a sampling arm that doubled as an emergency support whenever another vehicle encountered difficulties. The Sea Fleas contributed to rapid advancement in ocean understanding, especially the study of underwater ecosystems.

using the diving saucer. He combined this film with the footage collected by his son Philippe. Cousteau showed this footage to Melvin Payne, the executive producer of *National Geographic*. Payne became very enthusiastic and pitched the film to the CBS TV broadcasting company. CBS agreed to buy the film and broadcast it as a one-hour special to be aired in April 1966. They called it *The Undersea World of Jacques Cousteau*, with famed actor Orson Welles narrating. When David L. Wolper, a successful film and TV producer, watched the show from his home in Los Angeles, he was struck by an idea: Why not produce a whole television series about Cousteau's adventures?

Wolper traveled to France to meet Cousteau and present this idea. The format would be similar each week: a question would be raised at the start of the program, and then Cousteau and his team would set sail on *Calypso* to find the answer. The questions would be based on possible misconceptions about the sea, or seek answers to common questions regarding the mysteries of the deep. The show would also examine environmental issues, and how important it was to protect the delicate balance of life under the sea. It would give Cousteau a platform to educate people about both the sea and the importance of protecting it.

Producing the project, however, was difficult. First, *Calypso* needed to be cleaned and updated. Wolper also wanted the divers to be equipped with new diving gear that would look as modern and intriguing as the spacesuits astronauts wore. At this time, space exploration was on everyone's mind, and Wolper knew they'd have to figure out a way to make undersea exploration seem at least as exciting and interesting as going to the moon—a task that would not be easy.

By now, Cousteau's sons were grown up. While Philippe had followed in his father's footsteps and found a love for filming and diving, Jean-Michel was more of a businessperson and preferred to stay in the background, in comparison to his gregarious father and brother. Even so, their life and work on *Calypso* united them so that they all worked together to make the television project a success. In a twist of fate, Cousteau struck an unusual deal with another powerful man in the television industry. His name was Tom Moore and he worked for the ABC television network. He was also the president of the Explorers Club, an exclusive club with a famous membership list. When Cousteau and Wolper first pitched their idea for a series to Moore, he had failed to respond. Then one evening, Moore called Wolper and said he desperately needed a speaker for the Explorers Club. Wolper saw a chance to make a deal with Moore. If Cousteau came and spoke, would Moore persuade ABC to air 12 episodes of Cousteau's underwater series? Remarkably, Moore agreed and the deal was set.

The *Calypso* crew went into action to get the boat ready for the series. *Calypso* needed to be cleaned, painted, and newly outfitted for the demands of filming and traveling all over the world. Now, rather than being a research ship, *Calypso* would be a production set. Its research lab was turned into a dark room for developing film.

While Philippe joined his parents on *Calypso* to film the series, Jean-Michel stayed in Los Angeles to serve as their public

THE COUSTEAU SOCIETY

After his ABC TV series ended, Cousteau created the Cousteau Society for the Protection of Ocean Life with his sons and Frederick Hyman, a business consultant from Connecticut. A nonprofit company, the Cousteau Society was dedicated to advancing ocean research. The society set up a fundraising and membership campaign. Most people made donations of $20, while others mentioned the society in their wills. Thousands had been moved by *The Undersea World of Jacques Cousteau* and had come to love and care about the world's oceans and their precious resources. Cousteau had been right to believe that people would care about the sea once they saw the amazing life within it. In just the first year of the society's existence, more than 120,000 people gave an average of $20 each to become members. Today, the society continues to explore and observe ecosystems all over the world. It has educated millions of people about sea life and conservation.

The society's headquarters is located in Hampton, Virginia. Visitors can view a gallery where photos and artifacts from Cousteau's expeditions are displayed. The Cousteau Society has been the leader in developing underwater technology, submarines, imaging systems, underwater habitats, and many other systems to help scientists study sea life and share their findings with the world. Still, the society's primary focus is to educate the public on how to protect and manage the world's natural resources.

representative in the United States and to take care of business matters. He was also responsible for setting up a new underwater exploration exhibit to help introduce people to the sea and Jacques Cousteau's travels.

During a press conference to announce the new ABC series, Cousteau said that his mission was to educate the world about the sea and to help prevent the deterioration of the world's oceans, which was caused by pollution and overfishing, a bold statement at the time. For Cousteau, taking on the role of an environmentalist was more important than his role as Cousteau the adventurer or "manfish." He knew this opportunity was far more important than a chance to simply launch his film career. It was a chance to educate the world and perhaps save his beloved oceans.

The Undersea World of Jacques Cousteau stayed on the air for eight years. Cousteau and his team filmed sharks, whales, dolphins, sunken treasure, and coral reefs, producing 36 episodes in all. The series reached audiences all over the world, educating them about the ocean's natural treasures and the effects of pollution. The show starred Cousteau, his sons, and several crew members. The series made Cousteau a household name. He narrated each program and his soothing voice with its heavy French accent became instantly recognizable. In all, his documentaries have garnered 40 Emmy nominations and 10 Emmy awards.

Most importantly, the experience changed Cousteau's outlook and ambition dramatically. In his book *The Ocean World,* Cousteau writes, "Our 'liquid future' depends upon the foresight, care, and love with which we will manage our only water supply: the oceans."

A New Ship Sets Sail

Once the ABC series was over, Cousteau needed to find a new project. He wanted to create a new series that focused even more on conservation. One failed attempt was *Oasis in Space*. The series proposal was accepted by PBS, the newly-formed Public Broadcasting System, which was a nonprofit television network. In this new series, Cousteau hoped to reveal to the world the truth about environmental disasters, not just those taking place in the sea, but those happening all over the world. It would focus on the effects of ocean pollution, world hunger, overpopulation, chemical waste, and other threats to the environment. Raising the money for such an ambitious project would require sponsorship by wealthy businesses. However, these businesses were concerned that the series would affect their public image by exposing their own role in polluting the planet.

Despite these challenges, Cousteau was convinced that the series would be a success and felt it was the right thing to do. People needed to see with their own eyes the effects of pollution on the world. To fund the first episode, he used money from the

Cousteau Society's treasury. Even though the first episode won Cousteau an Emmy award, TV ratings were low. People were a bit turned off by it because rather than focusing on adventure, as the first series did, this new series focused on the devastation taking place.

Because of the low ratings, Cousteau had trouble finding a new sponsor to fund another episode. He realized that in order to create a successful series that achieved his goal, he had to figure out a way to make it appealing to audiences. As he did in his first series, he'd have to strike a balance between entertainment, education, and inspiration. Now dedicated more than ever to help to preserve the Earth's environment, he was determined to continue his work, no matter the obstacles. He had always been able to come up with ways to achieve the seemingly impossible, and this situation was no different.

COUSTEAU'S ODYSSEY

Finally, an oil man named Robert Anderson came to the rescue. Anderson was the chairman of the Atlantic Richfield Petroleum Company (ARCO). While Anderson seemed like an unlikely sponsor (since oil companies were one of the main contributors to water pollution and a key target of Cousteau's campaign), he wanted to improve his company's reputation so it would stand out among the other big oil companies. In other words, he thought it would be good publicity. Cousteau and Anderson entered into a deal.

The new series would be titled *The Jacques Cousteau Odyssey,* and it would become a popular PBS program. One early episode was called "Time Bomb at Fifty Fathoms," and its subject was sunken ships that contained dangerous cargo. To illustrate this danger, Cousteau investigated a recent collision between two ships that took place between the Italian and Albanian coasts on July 14, 1974. One of the ships, *Cavtat,* was carrying 900 50-gallon (189 liter) drums of tetramethyl lead (TML) and had sunk 300 feet (91.5 m) to the bottom.

TML is an extremely dangerous and deadly substance. When ingested, it attacks the body's central nervous system, making it difficult to breathe and control muscles, among other damaging effects. When the ship sank, many of the barrels broke, leaking TML into the water. Sea creatures in the area began to die. Their bodies rose to the surface in the huge oil slick that also resulted from the crash. Italian villagers became afraid to eat the fish, which they depended on for their livelihood.

Cousteau decided to write an article about this disaster for the *Saturday Review*. The article resulted in increased pressure on the Italian government to take action. They agreed to pay $12 million to retrieve the remaining barrels before they corroded and leaked more TML. Cousteau was on hand to film it all. At this moment, like so many others in his career, he recognized his power and influence. By the end of the project, only 3 percent of the poison remained in the sea. The episode was a huge success and helped promote the Cousteau Society's mission: inspiring the world to clean up its oceans.

LOSING PHILIPPE

Now that his new TV series was underway, Cousteau decided to invest in a small twin-engine sea plane which would allow the crew to travel to different shooting sites more quickly, and also allow them to reach places *Calypso* couldn't. They named the plane *Flying Calypso*. Philippe Cousteau, who followed in his father's footsteps in so many ways, loved to fly just like his father. He earned his pilot's license and became the plane's chief pilot. Father and son often flew together, and Cousteau was pleased to see that his son shared his love of flying. Philippe became a co-star in the new series.

Then, tragedy struck. On June 28, 1979, Philippe was flying the plane over Lisbon, Portugal, planning to land on the Tagus River. The plane, containing Philippe, a co-pilot, and six passengers, was about to land when something went wrong. It landed on the water at the wrong angle and flipped over, ejecting everyone but Philippe out of the plane, which sank instantly. Search crews spent two days searching for Philippe's body. Jacques and Simone Cousteau arrived to help with the search, along with Philippe's pregnant wife, Jan, and their young daughter, Alexandra. Jean-Michel Cousteau arrived, too. Other friends, along with the media, also gathered.

Philippe Cousteau worked closely with his father and was nominated for an Emmy for his underwater camerawork on "The Singing Whale" episode of the 1973 TV show *The Undersea World of Jacques Cousteau.*

A Portuguese military helicopter scoured the river for signs of Philippe. Several Navy divers joined the search as well. However, the river was muddy, making it hard to find anything, and when they finally found the plane, Philippe's body wasn't there. After three days, Philippe's remains were found trapped underwater.

After Philippe's funeral, Cousteau declared that the production of the *Jacques Cousteau Odyssey* would continue. He never spoke publicly of his son again, but published a letter to him in one of the reports to the Cousteau Society. In it, he wrote of an afternoon he'd spent flying with Philippe:

"I saw your shining face, proud to have something to give back to me, and I smiled because I knew that pursuing rainbows in your plane, you would always seek after the vanishing shapes of a better world."

BUILDING A NEW *CALYPSO*

Meanwhile, times were changing for *Calypso*. Cousteau decided that the United States was the best central location for him and his crew to continue the Cousteau Society's work. He decided to move *Calypso*'s home port from Monaco to Norfolk, Virginia. Jean-Michel Cousteau, who had become a well-known lecturer on environmental issues, took over Philippe's role in helping his father run the Cousteau Society and the family business.

By the early 1980s, there was a lot of discussion about alternative energy sources following the oil shortages of the 1970s. For a long time, Cousteau had been pondering the design of a ship that would be powered by the wind—not the way a sailboat travels, but with a wind-powered modern engine. By now, *Calypso* had been serving the crew for 30 wonderful years, but the boat was showing its age. Cousteau decided it was time to replace it with a newer, modern boat that was more environmentally friendly. Before Philippe died, the two often discussed building a wind-powered engine. Now, it seemed it was time to put another of Cousteau's ideas on paper and start work with designers to make it happen.

Jean-Michel Cousteau (*left*) talks with his father and others docked aboard *Calypso* while on an Amazon expedition in 1981.

Harnessing the Wind

Cousteau wasn't the only one looking for more fuel-efficient ways to power a boat. For decades, engineers had been trying to propel sea-going vessels using a wind-powered rotating metal cylinder, but so far they hadn't had any success. Cousteau decided to gather a team of engineers to keep trying. Cousteau first contacted Lucien Malavard, a professor of aeronautics at the Mechanics Institute in Paris. Together, they submitted a grant request to the French government to design a rotor sail. A rotor sail was a device with blades that would be erected on a ship's mast. It would work like a windmill, turned by the wind to produce power. Because of great concern about oil shortages and their huge economic impact on the economy, the French government decided to award one million dollars to Cousteau's project.

Cousteau and Malavard contacted A. R. Pechiney, who ran a metals company. Pechiney agreed to help build the prototype as long as the boat was made out of aluminum, which is what his company produced. Cousteau presented his plans for what he and Malavard called a Turbosail to Pechiney, who liked what he saw. However, because he was investing so much of his own product, Pechiney wanted to own the patent. Cousteau agreed to this, but altered the deal so that the Cousteau Society would earn a certain percentage of the royalties earned from the patent.

The First Test

The following year, Cousteau went to Toulouse to see a demonstration of a working Turbosail that Malabard had designed. Pechiney was there, too, along with many of his company's business executives. The Turbosail was 44 feet (13.5 m) tall, and made of aluminum. In many ways, the Turbosail had the same aerodynamic design as an airplane wing.

After studying the prototype, Cousteau was convinced it would work. He purchased a catamaran that was 65 feet (19.8 m) long. Malabard installed the Turbosail on its foredeck. They tested the boat, which Cousteau named *Moulin à Vent* ("Windmill"), in the Mediterranean. *Moulin à Vent* was able to reach a speed of 11.5 miles per hour (10 knots) without the assistance of any secondary engines. When the testing was complete, and Cousteau felt confident that *Moulin à Vent* was ready for its first voyage, he set sail in October 1983, planning to sail the boat from Tangier to New York. On board the ship was Cousteau, his son Jean-Michel, and a crew of five men (including a cameraman).

All went well for the first five days, but as they neared the southeast end of Bermuda, their luck changed. *Moulin à Vent* sailed into a gale, with winds of about 58 miles per hour (50 knots) and sea swells rising 20 feet (6 m). As the boat was tossed about, the Turbosail began to tear loose. Cousteau quickly turned off the Turbosail's rotor and secured it to the boat, using the backup motors to sail into Bermuda to make repairs. Again, the boat set sail for New York. They were just one day from reaching their destination when they hit rough seas again. This time, the Turbosail broke off the deck completely and fell into the sea.

Even though this trip was a disappointment, Cousteau would not be discouraged from his goal. At least he knew the Turbosail worked. Now, it was a matter of coming up with a design that would withstand the challenges of the sea. Next time, he would make an even bigger ship, with two Turbosails instead of one. There was only one problem: Cousteau needed more funding.

A NEW BUSINESS PARTNER

In 1983, John Denver, the famous singer and songwriter, talked with Cousteau about an up-and-coming businessman named Ted Turner. Turner was buying television stations to create his new cable network, the Turner Broadcasting System. Denver thought Cousteau and Turner might hit it off and urged Cousteau to see if Turner would be interested in sponsoring a new series.

At this time, Cousteau was about 73 years old. The Cousteau Society was about $5 million in debt. In somewhat the same way that Cousteau had been a pioneer of underwater filmmaking, Turner was a pioneer of cable television. Cousteau described his concerns about the world's rivers to Turner. He said that the world's rivers were becoming toxic sewers, and he convinced Turner to take on a project that would involve six months of traveling along the Amazon River. Cousteau proposed four one-hour long television specials at a cost of $6 million. Turner put out his hand to shake on it on the spot. Cousteau was back in business. In addition, the Cousteau Society had retained the rights to the PBS series, *The Jacques Cousteau Odyssey*. Cousteau offered to sell the rights to that program for an additional $5 million to Turner's company to which Turner agreed. Next, the Cousteau Society got to work putting together a team of 50 employees to produce the series.

Without the Turbosail, *Moulin à Vent* was useless, so *Calypso* was called back into action again. The ship was repaired and re-outfitted with new rudders and propellers, as well as many other fixes, including rebuilt engines.

Jacques Cousteau had a long, strong working relationship with Ted Turner, chairman of the board and president of Turner Broadcasting System. Here, Cousteau and Turner (*right*) speak at a conference in January 1992.

The new project's main goal was to explore the effect of human habitation on the Amazon River and its watersheds. Cousteau also wanted to show how watersheds were connected to the oceans and the impact that polluted rivers had not only on the communities that relied on them for food, water, and farming, but on the oceans they emptied into.

Cousteau chose the Amazon because it carries more than 20 percent of the Earth's freshwater to the Atlantic. The river is 4,000 miles (6,437 km) long. The threatened Amazon basin was a perfect example of how the activities of the human population were affecting the ecosystem. Timber harvesting and agribusiness had grown in the area, which led to increased population, and thus pollution.

FILMING THE "BIG MUDDY"

Another project Cousteau suggested to Turner was one that would focus on a river in the United States. He recommended a river that was closer to Ted Turner's home and heart: the Mississippi. Turner gave the green light and the team headed out on *Calypso* a month later. The crew was to spend a whole year sailing up the Mississippi, which is 2,300 miles (3,702 km) long. Along the way, in addition to filming, they planned to take water and other samples to measure pollution.

The Mississippi River, nicknamed "Big Muddy," was difficult to film underwater, for reasons its nickname suggests. However, like the project on the Amazon, Cousteau and his son, Jean-Michel, who was working on the project, wanted to focus not just on the environment, but on the lives of those who lived along the riverfront. As the crew traveled along the river, they interviewed the residents along the way. At each big city, huge parties were thrown in Cousteau's honor. As a result, the trip began to feel more like a publicity tour than a research expedition. By now, Cousteau and *Calypso* were extremely famous and their presence drew huge crowds.

The team produced two films from their trip in 1985: *Cousteau Mississippi: The Mississippi–Friendly Foe* and *Cousteau Mississippi: The Mississippi–Reluctant Ally*. *Reluctant Ally* won an Emmy Award for outstanding informational special.

While the filming itself was a miserable experience for almost everyone involved (several of the crew contracted malaria), it was all worth it in the end. The resulting film captured the devastating impact of human habitation on the Amazon, and in particular on the rain forests of Brazil. It showed how pollution from gold-mines in the Andes wound up in nearby streams that eventually fed into the Amazon, as well as how pollution released from the oil refineries into the air affected the rainfall hundreds of miles downriver. It was a film that showed every aspect of pollution—from its creation to its devastating effects. When Ted Turner saw the footage, he was thrilled with the powerful images and message.

TURBOSAIL, TAKE TWO

When Cousteau wasn't aboard *Calypso* for the Mississippi trip, he was travelling to Paris to continue work on the Turbosail project. Even though the first attempt was a failure, Cousteau was convinced that with the proper design it would work. This time, rather than trying to attach a Turbosail to an existing vessel, the entire ship was built from scratch. Cousteau completed the new ship in the summer

Cousteau's wind-powered catamaran with twin turbosails is shown docked in Cape Town, South Africa.

of 1985. Named *Alcyone,* after the daughter of Aeolus, the Greek god of the winds, the boat was twice as big as *Moulin à Vent.* It was 103 feet (31.3 m) long and built of aluminum. It had a wide beam, similar to a racing sailboat, and a catamaran stern for stability.

It also had two Turbosails instead of one—one mounted on the foredeck, the other mounted amidships. The Turbosails could propel the ship close to 14 miles per hour (12 knots), as long as there was a crosswind. On days when there wasn't enough wind, a computer-controlled diesel engine kicked in to keep the boat sailing at the same speed. *Alcyone* would only use from 60 to 70 percent

PARC OCÉANIC COUSTEAU

In the summer of 1988, an interactive amusement park, *Parc Océanique Cousteau,* opened in the Les Halles district in Paris. Jean-Michel Cousteau was in charge of the project, which was mainly funded by the Cousteau Society. To enter the park, visitors traveled in an elevator made to look and feel like a rocket in space diving into the depths of the ocean. The park included a life-size replica of Jacques Cousteau, which would answer questions in a pre-recorded voice. Visitors could also walk around inside a full-size replica of a blue whale and touch reproductions of its organs. The park had a theater with a 45-foot screen on which Cousteau's films were shown. One unique aspect of the park is that it didn't keep any live animals in captivity. It was considered the world's first high-tech *oceanarium.* The Cousteaus had high hopes for the park and its unique modern conception. However, by 1994, the technology in the park was already becoming obsolete and it closed. Still, the park was, like nearly all of Cousteau's endeavors, a challenging and unique project that set it apart from all others.

of the fuel a normal boat of the same size would use. Cousteau declared that this boat would cross the Atlantic successfully.

The crew was optimistic as they set sail, but they soon discovered a design flaw relating to comfort. Even in slightly rough seas, the boat rocked and tipped so much, it made the entire crew seasick. Nevertheless, the boat itself stayed intact during the voyage to New York. The Cousteau Society arranged for a huge welcome in the New York harbor. They timed the arrival so that *Calypso* could sail along with *Alcyone* into harbor. A huge crowd of up to 10,000 people waited to cheer on the boats and their hero, Jacques Cousteau. The mayor of New York, Edward I. Koch, issued an official proclamation, promoting Cousteau from captain to admiral.

A few days later, Cousteau and several of his crew sailed *Calypso* to Washington, D.C. via Chesapeake Bay, and then up the Potomac River. There, President Ronald Reagan presented Cousteau with the Medal of Freedom—the highest decoration a civilian can receive from the U.S. government—for Cousteau's work in revealing the mysteries of the ocean to the world.

Return to the Sea

In 1991, one of Ted Turner's cable television networks aired the
Amazon series, which was called *Journey to a Thousand Rivers*.
It was time to decide on a new project. Now that Jacques Cousteau
was in his eighties, his next project might be the one to stand as his
legacy, and so he and Jean-Michel both wanted it to be as meaning-
ful as it could be.

They presented their new idea to Turner: This trip would retrace
the same routes taken by famous early explorers, such as Hernando
Cortés, Ferdinand Magellan, Amerigo Vespucci, and Ponce de
Leon. They would call the series *Jacques Cousteau's Rediscovery of
the World*. Both *Calypso* and *Alcyone* would embark on a five-year
expedition that would take them through the Panama Canal and
around Cape Horn to the Pacific, then over to New Zealand and
Australia. The final part of their journey would take them up the
great rivers of Asia.

Along the way, the team would document how humans inter-
acted with the Earth's rivers and oceans. Cousteau wanted to
explore the effect of farming on the rivers and seas, and how cattle

Jacques Cousteau (*second from left*) and son Jean-Michel (*second from right*) receive certificates of honor from Academy for Television Arts and Sciences President Leo Chaloukian (*left*) in January 1992. Also in the picture is long-time Cousteau friend and producer David L. Wolper.

waste running into the ocean was affecting the plant and animal life in the Great Barrier Reef. Finally, Cousteau would show how land creatures were affecting the creatures who lived in our most precious resource—water.

Cousteau and his son set up a meeting with Turner to pitch their idea. When they were done, Turner was quiet. The Cousteaus held their breath as they waited for Turner to make a decision. The room fell unbearably silent before Turner finally said yes.

When the boats set sail, *Calypso* had a crew of 26 men plus Simone Cousteau, while *Alcyone* had a crew of 11 men. Cousteau himself spent little time onboard. Instead, he traveled from country to country, giving lectures to raise money and spread the word about the deterioration of the world's oceans. Cousteau believed that all

Cousteau poses with his wife Francine in April 1995.

countries should be moving toward the use of solar power as an energy source, noting that eventually the world would run out of resources such as coal and oil for fuel.

Ever since his son Philippe died, Cousteau and his wife had grown apart. Cousteau had met a woman named Francine Triplet in Paris and began a secret relationship with her. They eventually had two children, Diane and Pierre Yves. Often when Cousteau wasn't filming his TV series, he would travel back to Paris to be with his secret family. Around this time, in 1990, Simone Cousteau learned that she had an aggressive form of cancer and so returned to *Calypso* to live out her final days on the boat she loved and on which she had spent her entire adult life. After her death on December 1, 1990, her ashes were scattered in the Mediterranean Sea.

After Simone's death, Cousteau told Jean-Michel about his relationship with Francine Triplet and said he planned to marry her. Jean-Michel was shocked to learn that he had two half-siblings.

WHO OWNS THE COUSTEAU NAME?

After he left the family business, Jean-Michel Cousteau sought out other business ventures. He lectured quite frequently, but he was also interested in a new, eco-friendly resort that was being planned for construction in the Fijian islands. The resort would have very strict rules in regard to the environment; for example, guests were not allowed to use Jet Skis or motorboats. Fishing would also be prohibited. Instead, guests would be encouraged to enjoy the beauty of the sea through such activities as scuba diving and snorkeling. Because of these policies, ones that were also strongly in line with his father's convictions, Jean-Michel decided to get involved. He was shocked, however, when his own father sued him after discovering that Jean-Michel wanted to advertise the resort as a "Cousteau environmental resort." Cousteau dropped the suit when Jean-Michel agreed he would use his full name to advertise and describe his business or nonprofit ventures. The resort became the "Jean-Michel Cousteau Fiji Islands Resort." Later, Jean-Michel, who was now as devoted to conservation as his father, founded his own conservation organization called Ocean Futures Society. In May 2010, he published a book with National Geographic about growing up as the son of Jacques Cousteau, *My Father the Captain: My Life With Jacques Cousteau.*

After settling some business deals with his father, Jean-Michel decided to leave the family business. Now that Cousteau had a new family, he had to decide what to do next. He hired his new wife as a screenwriter and began to acquaint her with the many facets of his business and his work as an environmentalist.

SAYING GOOD-BYE TO A LEGEND

At age 85, Cousteau became ill with lung cancer. He continued to do some interviews, still eager to spread the word about his concerns for the planet and the dire need for humans to take care of it.

Investigators survey the partially sunken Calypso at Singapore's Kwong Soon shipyard in January 1996. The ship, which had been at the shipyard since September 24, 1994, sank in shallow water.

Then, on January 11, 1996, he experienced another unexpected disappointment when *Calypso* sank. The boat was in Singapore, being prepared for a final voyage back to France, where it would be retired from service, when a barge that had drifted loose rammed into it. *Calypso* sank in 16 feet (4.8 m) of water. All that was visible above the surface was the mast, crow's nest, and foredeck. Cousteau's old friend, Albert Falco, arranged to have the boat pulled from the water and hauled onto a barge headed for Marseille.

By now, Cousteau was very ill. As *Calypso* was being taken home, Cousteau suffered a heart attack. He died two days later, on June 25, 1997.

Cousteau's funeral was held at the Cathedral of Notre Dame. Thousands of mourners came to pay their respects. The archbishop of Paris gave the mass. French president Jacques Chirac spoke, as did Jacques Cousteau's son, Jean-Michel. Cousteau was buried next to his parents in a cemetery at St.-André-de-Cubzac. The tomb faces northwest, toward the Gironde Estuary and the ocean.

RESTORING CALYPSO

Both Jacques and Simone Cousteau had requested that *Calypso* be sunk if ever there came a time when it was no longer possible to repair the boat. Neither of them could stand the thought of *Calypso* becoming a simple tourist attraction. Still, after their deaths, neither Cousteau's second wife, Francine Triplet, nor his son Jean-Michel Cousteau could bear to let the ship go, especially since *Calypso* had come to mean so much to so many people around the world. *Calypso* had served many functions in its 60-plus years on the sea: a minesweeper, a ferry, an oceanic research vessel, and, finally, an icon for environmental protection. *Calypso* may have originally been created for the purpose of war, but under the Cousteau family and crew, the boat had become a symbol of peace and the protection of Earth's environment.

Jean-Michel and Francine fought many legal battles over ownership of *Calypso*. The Cousteau Society was never actually the legal owner of *Calypso*. The boat had been leased to Cousteau, and later to his society, by Loel Guinness, and that arrangement had remained in place for the past 50 years. Finally, Loel Guinness's grandson and heir sold *Calypso* to the Cousteau Society, again for the symbolic amount of one French franc. They were given full rights to restore the boat, which began on October 12, 2007. Since Jean-Michel Cousteau had been cut off from the Society after his mother's death, the restoration was now the responsibility of Cousteau's second wife.

Francine Triplet Cousteau organized the restoration of *Calypso*, which took place at the Piriou shipyard in Concarneau, Brittany, France. The boat was to be completely refurbished and sail again as an ambassador for the seas and oceans. To get the vessel to the shipyard, the topsides and bridge needed to be lined with plywood sheets. These helped prevent leakage and reinforced the structure of the ship. The ship was pulled into the shipyard by two tugboats and assisted by a technical ship so a crew could be on hand to make repairs if anything went wrong.

At the Piriou shipyard, *Calypso* was given a total makeover. The bridge was dismantled. The ship was stripped down to its skeleton. Once the skeleton was reinforced, reconstruction began. The "false nose," which was the underwater observation chamber Cousteau designed, was rebuilt and reattached.

The plans called for *Calypso* to become a "green ship." It was originally built in 1942 from Oregon pine, but the new ship would be made from oak and larch from forests managed by the Office National des Forêts (National Forestry Office). Any trees cut for the project would be replaced right away to ensure the tree harvest was sustainable.

The engines would have the cleanest possible injectors. Instead of using polyurethane for the hull, hemp oakum, which is made from burnt sienna and linseed oil, would be used to coat the hemp (the caulking for the hull). Instead of using epoxy and silica (toxic materials) for dowels in the nail holes in the planking, wooden plugs would be used.

Jean-Michael Cousteau, with daughter Celine and son Fabien, prepares to dive as part of celebration festivities to celebrate the 100th birthday of Jacques Cousteau in Marseille, France, in June 2010.

The plans were set. However, in February 2009, before the restoration could be completed, funding for it ran out and plans were put on hold. Then, on June 8, 2010, BBC News reported that *Calypso* was to be relaunched during the year-long celebration to mark the centennial of Cousteau's birth.

THE LEGACY OF JACQUES COUSTEAU

Jacques Cousteau lived a full and exciting life, and each chapter of it led him to a deeper understanding and appreciation of the world's most precious resource: water. He was a French naval officer, ocean-ographer, inventor, environmentalist, explorer, filmmaker, adven-turer, innovator, inventor, photographer, author, filmmaker, father and friend to anyone who cared to listen as he stood proudly in his red woolen cap and told stories of the sea—its past, its present, and his hopes for its future. His influence on our understanding and regard for the sea and all of its remarkable creatures is unmatched. Cousteau was the first to open a window into the silent world of Earth's oceans. He never wavered in his love for adventure and edu-cation. His books and films shaped humanity's view of undersea life. His inventions revolutionized undersea exploration and research. Cousteau remains the most famous oceanic conservationist in his-tory. His legacy lives on every time a young diver straps on scuba gear and dives underwater for the first time, entering the silent world that Cousteau loved so dearly.

How to Get Involved

These sites provide resources to gain information about how to get involved in conservation and ocean-related issues.

The Green Squad

http://www.nrdc.org/greensquad

This organization for children and teens is part of the National Resources Defense Council. This site provides information on how to be more eco-friendly at school and in daily life.

The Cousteau Society

www.cousteau.org

Founded by Jacques Cousteau in 1973, The Cousteau Society works to educate the public about environmental issues and to help influence policy makers to make informed decisions on issues that could affect the planet.

Ocean Futures Society

http://www.oceanfutures.org

Founded by Jean-Michel Cousteau, the society's goal is to explore the Earth's oceans and to inspire and educate people to act responsibly to protect them.

Chronology

June 11, 1910	Jacques Cousteau is born in Saint-André-de-Cubzac, Gironde, France.
July 12, 1937	Jacques Cousteau marries Simone Melchior.
1938	Cousteau's first son, Jean-Michel, is born.
1940	Cousteau's second son, Philippe, is born.
1942	Cousteau shoots his first film, *Dix-huit Metres de Fond* ("Ten Fathoms Down"), using a 35 mm Kinamo Camera in a watertight case.
1942	Cousteau collaborates with Émile Gagnan to perfect the Aqua-Lung, the first underwater breathing apparatus.
1943	Cousteau uses the Aqua-Lung to film *Épaves* ("Shipwreck").
1946	Cousteau's brother, Pierre-Antoine, is condemned to die for his anti-Semitic writings in the newspaper *Je Suit Partout* ("I Am Everywhere"). He is later given a lesser sentence to life in prison, but is released in 1954.
1948	Cousteau works with Phillip Tailliez, Frédéric Dumas, Jean Alinat, and Marcel Ichac to set up the first underwater archaeology operation.
1950	Cousteau founds the French Oceanographic Campaigns (FOC).
1951	Cousteau leases *Calypso,* a navy minesweeper that he would convert to a floating laboratory for explorations all over the world.
1953	Cousteau publishes his first book, *The Silent World: A Story of Undersea Discovery and Adventure.*

1955	*Calypso* is outfitted with an underwater, glass observation chamber, the first of its kind.
1955	Cousteau films *The Silent World*.
1956	Cousteau wins the Palme d'Or at the Cannes Film Festival for *The Silent World*.
1957	Cousteau resigns from the Navy, becomes elected as director of the Oceanographical Museum of Monaco and is admitted to the U.S. National Academy of Sciences.
1959	Along with Jean Mollard, Cousteau develops *La Soucoupe Plongeante* ("The Diving Saucer"), the first underwater vehicle designed specifically for scientific undersea exploration.
March 28, 1960	*Time Magazine* puts Cousteau on their cover to acknowledge his work and attendance at the World Oceanic Congress.
1960	Cousteau organizes a successful protest to help stop the French Atomic Energy Commission from dumping atomic waste into the Mediterranean Sea.
1961	*National Geographic* presents Cousteau with their gold medal at a White House ceremony hosted by President John F. Kennedy.
1962	Cousteau develops Conshelf I, the first manned undersea colony off Marseilles, France.
1963	Cousteau develops Conshelf II in the Red Sea.
1964	Cousteau films *World Without Sun*, a documentary about five men who live in Conshelf II for one month.
1965	Cousteau develops Conshelf III outside Nice, France.

1966   The first hour-long television special called *The World of Jacques-Yves Cousteau* aired to high ratings, landing Cousteau a contract with ABC for the series *The Undersea World of Jacques Cousteau,* which would first air in 1968.

1967   The Cousteau team develops "sea fleas"—tiny submersibles that can hold one person and reach underwater depths of up to 1,000 feet (350 meters).

1968   Cousteau's television series, *The Undersea World of Jacques Cousteau,* makes its debut.

1973   Cousteau founds the Cousteau Society for the Protection of Ocean Life.

1975   Cousteau and his crew uncover the wreck of the hospital ship *Britannic* near the Greek island of Kea in the Aegean Sea.

1977   Cousteau and Peter Scott are co-recipients of the United Nations International Environment Prize.

1979   Cousteau's son Philippe dies in a plane crash.

1980   Cousteau's third child, Diane, is born (to mother Francine Triplet).

1980   Cousteau travels to the Saint Lawrence River and the Great Lakes in Canada to film *Cries from the Deep* and *St. Lawrence: Stairway to the Sea.*

1980   Cousteau helps develop the Turbosail, a ship powered mainly by a wind turbine.

1982   Cousteau's fourth child, Pierre-Yves, is born (to mother Francine Triplet).

1985	Cousteau receives the Presidential Medal of Freedom from Ronald Reagan.
	He also publishes another book, *The Ocean World*.
1989	Cousteau is inducted into the French Academy.
1990	Cousteau's first wife, Simone Melchior, dies of cancer.
1991	Cousteau marries Francine Triplet.
1992	Cousteau is the only non-politician to attend the Rio Summit, also called the "Earth Summit", the United Nations Conference on Environment and Development (UNCED).
January 11, 1996	*Calypso* is rammed by a barge in Singapore and sinks.
June 25, 1997	Cousteau dies at his home in Paris.

Glossary

amphorae   Ancient Greek or Roman jars, which usually have a narrow neck and two handles

Aqua-Lung   The first underwater breathing apparatus

Bathyscaphe   A manned submersible vessel; from the Greek words *bathus* (meaning "deep") and *skaphos* (referring to the hull of a ship); coined by inventor Auguste Piccard

crow's nest   A platform attached to the mast of a vessel, usually used as a lookout to provide a longer-range view

dirigible   A gas-filled airship with a rigid structure that is steered by rudders or propellers

dredge   An apparatus used to pull substances out of the water by scooping or dragging

enteritis   An inflammation of the small intestine

gyroscope   A navigation device for measuring orientation

jute   Plant fiber used to make twine or rope

minesweeper   A warship used to detect explosive mines

SCUBA   Acronym for self-contained *u*nderwater *b*reathing *a*pparatus

sea fleas   Tiny, one-man submersibles

Turbosail   A tall cylinder with a propeller at the top, used to power a ship

Bibliography

"Biography: Jacques-Yves Cousteau." Eastern Illinois University. 2005. http://www.eiu.edu/~wow/classes/fa05/cjbio.html. Accessed February 2010.

Burns, Christopher. "Jacques Cousteau Dies in Paris at 87." Associated Press via The Free Library. 1997. http://www.thefreelibrary.com/JACQUES+COUSTEAU+DIES+IN+PARIS+AT+87-a083872064. Accessed February 2010.

Campbell, Matthew. "*Calypso* Sails Free of Jacques Cousteau Feud." *The Sunday Times, UK*. January 27, 2008. http://www.timesonline.co.uk/tol/news/world/europe/article3257053.ece. Accessed April 2010.

Cousteau, Jacques. *Jacques Cousteau: The Ocean World*. New York: Harry N. Abrams, 1985.

Cousteau, Jacques and Frédéric Dumas. *The Silent World*. Washington, DC: National Geographic Adventure Classics, 1953, 2004.

Cousteau, Jacques and Susan Schiefelbein. *The Human, The Orchid, and the Octopus*. New York: Bloomsbury, 2007.

The Cousteau Society Web site. http://www.cousteau.org/. Accessed February 2010.

DuTemple, Lesley A. *Jacques Cousteau*. Minneapolis: Lerner Publications Company, 2000.

The Edgerton Digital Collections Project Web site. http://edgerton-digital-collections.org. Accessed July 2010.

Hartl, John. "Jacques Cousteau: The Sea King: A Life In and About The Sea." *The Seattle Times*. November 1, 2009. http://seattletimes.nwsource.com/html/books/2010171606_br01cousteau.html. Accessed March 2010.

"In Memory of a Great Environmentalist." Interview with Jacques Cousteau with Jim Motavalli in *The Environmental Magazine*. March 1, 1996. http://www.ecomall.com/activism/emag.htm. Accessed February 2010.

"Jacques Cousteau." *Encyclopedia of World Biography.* 2010. http://www.notablebiographies.com/Co-Da/Cousteau-Jacques.html. Accessed February 2010.

"Jacques Cousteau." Whitney R. Harris World Ecology Center. University of Missouri, St. Louis. http://icte.umsl.edu/WEArecipients/cousteau.html . Accessed February 2010.

"Jacques Cousteau: The Adventure Over." Online Newshour, PBS. June 25, 1997. http://www.pbs.org/newshour/bb/remember/1997/cousteau_6-25.html. Accessed February 2010.

"Jacques Cousteau's Ship Calypso is to be Relaunched." BBC News. June 8, 2010. http://news.bbc.co.uk/2/hi/science_and_environment/10264797.stm. Accessed July 2010.

"Jacques-Yves Cousteau." Cousteau Kids (The Cousteau Society). No pub date. http://www.cousteaukids.org/frm_cousteau.html. Accessed February 2010.

"Jean-Michel Cousteau." Ocean Futures Society. http://www.oceanfutures.org/about/jean-michel-cousteau. Accessed April 2010.

"Jean Michel Cousteau." *Encyclopedia of World Biography.* http://www.notablebiographies.com/supp/Supplement-Ca-Fi/Cousteau-Jean-Michel.html. Accessed April 2010.

"Jean-Michel Cousteau's Ocean Future Society." http://www.oceanfutures.org/. Accessed April 2010.

"Lucien Malavard (1910-1990)." Encyclopaedia Universalis. 2010. http://www.universalis.fr/encyclopedie/lucien-malavard/. Accessed July 2010.

Lundgren, Richard. "HMHS Britannic." Ocean Discovery. 1999. http://www.ocean-discovery.org/britannic.htm. Accessed February 2010.

Matson, Brad. *Jacques Cousteau: The Sea King.* New York: Pantheon Books, 2009.

Pickering, David. "Cousteau, Jacques: French Scientist/Television Producer." The Museum of Broadcast Communications, 2010. http://www.museum.tv/eotvsection.php?entrycode=cousteaujac. Accessed July 2010.

Salman, Rachel. "Jacques Cousteau." *SPECTRUM Home and School Magazine,* 2009. http://www.incwell.com/Biographies/Cousteau.html. Accessed February 2010.

Sanction, Thomas. "Jacques-Yves Cousteau: Lord of the Depths." *TIME.* March 29, 1999. http://www.time.com/time/magazine/article/0,9171, 990599,00.html. Accessed February 2010.

"Simone Melchior Cousteau." Ocean Futures Society. 2010. http://www. oceanfutures.org/about/cousteau-family/simone-melchior-cousteau. Accessed March 2010.

"Underwater Habitat." HowStuffWorks.com. October 29, 2008. http:// science.howstuffworks.com/underwater-habitat-info.htm#. Accessed April 2010.

Further Resources

BOOKS

Bankston, John. *Jacques-Yves Cousteau: His Story Under the Sea.* Hockessin: Mitchell Lane Publishers, 2002.

Desonie, Dana. *Oceans: How We Use the Seas (Our Fragile Planet).* New York: Chelsea House Publishers, 2007.

Ganeri, Anita. *Protecting Ocean Habitats (Protecting Habitats).* New York: Gareth Stevens Publishing, 2005.

Gerdes, Louise I. *Endangered Oceans: Opposing Viewpoints.* Farmington Hills: Greenhaven Press, 2009.

La Bella, Laura. *Not Enough to Drink: Pollution, Draught and Tainted Water Supplies.* New York: Rosen Publishing Group, 2009.

Spilsbury, Louise. *Water (Planet Under Pressure).* Chicago: Heinemann-Raintree, 2007.

Walker, Pam. *People and the Sea (Life in the Sea).* New York: Facts on File, 2005.

WEB SITES

Environmental Kids Club

www.epa.gov/kids

Presented by the U.S. Environmental Protection Agency, this is an interactive Web site for students who want to learn more about recycling and the environment.

Looking at the Sea

www.mos.org/oceans/planet/index.html

This interactive site is produced by the Museum of Science, Boston. Readers can learn about the physical features of the ocean, the water cycle and other interesting facts about the world's seas.

Cousteau Kids

www.cousteaukids.org

A branch of the Cousteau Society, Cousteau Kids is for ages 8 to 12. It helps students explore nature around the world through its magazine and Web site.

Ocean Futures Society

http://www.oceanfutures.org

This site includes resources for global education programs for young people, with information about the Cousteaus, information about current expeditions, and educational resources.

USGS Water Science for Schools

http://ga.water.usgs.gov/edu

The United States Geological Survey's Web site provides information about the oceans and conservation.

Picture Credits

Index

About the Author

JOHANNA KNOWLES has been writing nonfiction for children, teens, and adults for over ten years. She has a master's degree in children's literature from Simmons College and teaches writing for children at the Center for the Study of Children's Literature at Simmons College. She lives in Vermont with her husband and son.